Arsdell. November 1943.

To Father with Much Love

D0590578

6°

M. Hill

FROM DUSK TILL DAWN

Books by A. G. Street

FARMER'S GLORY
STRAWBERRY ROAN
HEDGE TRIMMINGS
COUNTRY DAYS
THE ENDLESS FURROW
THINKING ALOUD
LAND EVERLASTING
COUNTRY CALENDAR
FARMING : HOW TO BEGIN
THE GENTLEMAN OF THE PARTY
MOONRAKING
FARMING ENGLAND
ALREADY WALKS TO-MORROW
A YEAR OF MY LIFE
A CROOK IN THE FURROW
ROUND THE YEAR ON THE FARM
WESSEX WINS

FROM
DUSK TILL DAWN

By

A. G. STREET

GEORGE G. HARRAP & CO. LTD.
LONDON   TORONTO   BOMBAY   SYDNEY

TO

BRITAIN'S HOME GUARD

AND ESPECIALLY TO THOSE MEMBERS OF THIS
FORCE WHO WROUGHT SO FAITHFULLY AND SO
PATIENTLY WITH ONE WILTSHIRE FARMER

First published February 1943
by GEORGE G. HARRAP & CO. LTD.
182 High Holborn, London, W.C.1

Reprinted: June 1943; *September* 1943

THIS BOOK IS PRODUCED IN
COMPLETE CONFORMITY WITH THE
AUTHORIZED ECONOMY STANDARDS

Composed in Plantin type and printed by Morrison & Gibb, Ltd.
London and Edinburgh
Made in Great Britain

Contents

CHAPTER I

Dusk

U NFORTUNATELY my personal knowledge of the Continent is confined to one glorious week's holiday at Zoute, on the Belgian coast, in 1936, during which, in company with three good friends, I played much bad golf, drank gallons of lager beer, and had no end of fun. Still more unfortunately my experience of soldiering is nil. So, for the beginning of this book I am obliged to rely on the rather dull imagination of a farmer ; or, as, I hope, a good Home Guard, to make the best use of the materials at my disposal.

I have a notion that during the first week or so of May 1940 something like this must have happened somewhere in Northern France or Flanders. In some château, where the victorious German Army had established a temporary Field Headquarters Mess, the officers must have been congratulating their Führer and themselves on the amazing success of their attack to date. This must have led to speculation concerning the immediate future, and a general agreement that nothing could save the British Expeditionary Force from complete annihilation or capture. Having counted that unhatched chicken, the next on the list would have been the invasion and conquest of Britain ; and a free translation of the remarks of Colonel von This to Major von That might go something after this fashion.

" Once their army here is destroyed, Karl, it is the end. We shall invade and conquer their island with ease. It will be, as they say, a walk-over."

" But, Ludwig, they have an army at home, surely ? "

" No. It is inexplicable but true. They have nothing to defend their island, less than nothing. Our submarines will

7

keep their navy out of the Channel ; our glorious Luftwaffe will bomb London, the Channel Ports, and all the South of England into panic and submission ; and then our army will go through the whole of Britain like a knife through butter."

" Are you sure they have no real army at home, Ludwig ? "

" Positive.   They are a nation of fools who do not believe in armies.   There will be a few of their Territorial troops, a few *francs-tireurs*, and a few hysterical women with rifles, but of real fighting strength, nothing, Ludwig, less than nothing.   *Ach*, how I shall enjoy that trip ! "

That sort of conversation would have found few critics on the other side of the Channel, for there most men were criticizing themselves, and admitting that the recent defeat of the British Army and the almost certain probability of worse defeats in the immediate future were largely their responsibility.   The war was not a popular topic, for people were afraid.   They were haunted by the fear of Britain's defeat, and only when hard at work could they forget that fear.   Day by day the news from the Continent became worse and worse.   Newspapers published maps showing the rapid advance of the German mechanized divisions. Cabinet Ministers and broadcast commentators spoke at length in an attempt to gloss over the danger, and military correspondents wrote long articles in similar strain.

But everywhere in Britain, civilians, and especially middle-aged civilians, worried much and talked little.   Suddenly everything worth while was in the melting-pot of modern war, and they realized that they were too old to take a hand in the stirring.   All they possessed, all they had achieved, and all of which they were so proud were suddenly worth nothing, less than nothing.   And always their worrying brought the same conclusion—that the present hopeless state of things was largely their own fault.

From castle and cottage, in town and village, in factories and in fields, men went to work with fear and shame for

companions. Was this to be the end of Britain as a world
Power ? Was the downfall of the British Commonwealth
of Nations in sight ? Were the easy days of twenty years of
careless peace now to bring their logical harvest ? Was it
possible that the island of Britain, inviolate for so many
centuries, could be invaded and conquered ? If so, would
this mean the end of all decency in human life for many
generations ? The fear of these things was bad, but the
shame of knowing that they were the direct and logical
result of their own selfish carelessness and sloth was far
worse, and together these made up a heavy burden for every
man in Britain.

For there was no doubt about it, the German officer's
boast that once her army in France was destroyed, Britain
would be practically defenceless was true. The paucity of
the defence was only too obvious. A first-class navy with
its hands already more than full of trouble, a small first-
quality air force, and perhaps a few thousands of quarter-
trained troops. To repel a German invasion there was
nothing, indeed less than nothing, until the evening of
May 14, 1940, when the voice of the Secretary of State for
War suddenly came on the air. Here is the Press report of
that amazing broadcast :

In order to supplement, from sources as yet untapped,
the home defence of the country, it has been decided to
create a new force to be known as " Local Defence
Volunteers."
This force, which will be voluntary and unpaid, will
be open to British subjects between the ages of seventeen
and sixty-five years of age. The period of service will
be for the duration of the war. Volunteers accepted will
be provided with uniforms and will be armed.
Men of reasonable physical fitness and with a knowledge
of firearms should give in their names at their local police
stations. The need is greatest in small towns, villages,
and less densely populated areas. The duties of the

force can be undertaken in a volunteer's spare time. Members of existing Civil Defence organizations should consult their officers before registering under this scheme.

The force will be under the command of the General Officer Commanding-in-Chief, Home Forces.

The response to this appeal astonished everybody. There was no doubt that the rapid worsening of the war situation in France was one reason for this, but the major one was that this new volunteer force provided an opportunity for thousands of men to feel that at last they could do something to help their country in her hour of need. Ex-soldiers, now considered too old for fighting, could show that they were not too old. Lads of seventeen and middle-aged civilians could show that they were as good as the old soldiers. Civilians of military age who had been prevented from joining the services by reason of the value of their civilian work could now give their scanty leisure to training as part-time soldiers. Civilians, and there were many, who had never before shouldered a Service rifle and who hated the army and all its works, could now row in with the others, and in so doing, forget some of their prejudices and many of their fears.

Within a week more than a quarter of a million men had been enrolled, and the task of equipping and organizing this huge force almost overwhelmed the authorities. These difficulties were accentuated by a continuation of reverses in Northern France and the enemy's reaction to the news of the formation of this Local Defence force. The German authorities immediately announced that in the event of any of its members being captured with arms in their hands they would be treated as *francs-tireurs* and shot. It was clear that a detachable arm-band would not meet the situation, and that uniforms must be provided as quickly as possible.

But in every town and village in Britain the men who had enrolled in this new force were demanding not uniforms,

but arms, ammunition, and opportunities to use them.
Above all they demanded rifles, in order to keep safe watch
and ward over their own district, so that the tactics the Hun
had employed so successfully in Holland should not work
unhindered in Britain.

However, before either arms or uniforms could be provided it was first necessary to organize some form of
leadership and control of these new and enthusiastic Local
Defence Volunteers. From time out of mind Britain's
towns and villages had been divided, like all democracies,
into the people who did the work and the critics. Therefore, in the beginning the leadership of the L.D.V. passed
largely into the hands of the former section, previous
military experience being an added qualification.

As a countryman I can speak with certainty only for the
rural districts, where the natural choice of leader was usually
the local feudal overlord, who was appointed platoon
commander. Generally speaking, this gave him the command of anything from thirty to a hundred men ; and,
guided by his local knowledge, from these he picked his
junior commanders or section leaders. This selection was
usually a wise choice of ex-Service men and non-Service
men in the proportion of three to two ; but in almost every
case the main qualification was that the chosen man had
proved to his rural neighbours that he could run his business
adequately and also that he could be relied upon to shoulder
responsibility on his own.

These section leaders used the same yard-stick in selecting
their squad leaders ; and the occasional newcomer to the
countryside who suddenly found himself a platoon commander was amazed at the swift and accurate way in which
his section leaders sized up the quality of each newly
enrolled man. One such in my hearing accused his stalwarts
of running a private village Gestapo for years before.
" There's nothing you don't know about your neighbours,"

he protested. " It's useful—in fact, invaluable just now—but, damn it, it's indecent."

He had not been in the countryside long enough to realize that while a man may cover up his failings in a large community, he can never do so in a small one. For instance, while the town politician may hide his inefficiency for years under a cloak of clever talk and showmanship, no amount of either will cover up bad work on the part of the village house-thatcher.

Left Wing critics may argue that the original method of selecting leaders was both unwise and unfair, and that it must have handicapped the force with many indifferent officers ; but I, a countryman with more Left Wing tendencies than most, saw the rural L.D.V. from the word go, and I can think of no better way. The point to remember is that this huge force had been born in one night, that there was no organization to deal with it, and that the situation demanded that it should begin its duties as soon as possible. Admittedly, in the beginning there were bad choices of leaders and many mistakes, but the countryside and the L.D.V. itself soon weeded out the former and corrected the latter.

Anyway, in spite of its many weaknesses the method used did get the L.D.V. in action as an observation force in a surprisingly short time. In every district meetings of possible and probable leaders were held in order to discuss ways and means. At these conferences every section of rural society was represented. Owners of great estates rubbed shoulders with tenant farmers and small-holders. The ' county ' for once found itself talking eagerly and on terms of equality with the local retail trade. Ex-soldiers of every rank fought their old battles over again, and yearned aloud for new ones. The butcher, the grocer, the baker, the garage mechanic, the blacksmith, the thatcher, the gamekeeper, the farm worker, and even the poacher was represented. Half an hour before the appointed time it was usually a case of standing room only, with a loud buzz of conversation and a cloud of tobacco smoke dominating the village hall.

For within a few days of the Secretary of State's appeal a huge force had suddenly sprung into being, which by its size and enthusiasm threatened to defeat itself. To administer, train, and equip this force required a well-tried organization, and the existing military one was already strained almost to breaking-point by the rapidly worsening position of the British Army overseas. So the only possible hope was the County Territorial Army and Air Force Associations, and to them this gigantic task was entrusted.

These Associations now found themselves, with seriously depleted staffs, suddenly faced with the problem of administering a force many hundreds of thousands strong, which had, as it were, grown up overnight. This problem was not one of merely expanding an existing skeleton organization along well-tried lines. It was not even one of devising a new organization to deal with a definite, though large, volume of work. Instead, they now had to face the heart-breaking task of attempting to keep pace with a problem that would grow in size and difficulty each day, and for which there was no proved solution. It says much for the place that the Territorial Associations had won for themselves in the sphere of military organization in Britain that not only were they asked to do this strange yet important work, but also that they accepted the responsibility.

Naturally enough the Territorial Associations selected the leaders of this new force largely on their previous military experience, but for security reasons every member of the L.D.V., from zone commander to private, or rather to volunteer, had first to be approved by the local police. Frankly, it surprised many of them to learn how much the local police knew concerning the most law-abiding countryman.

At these district meetings it was decided that the chief responsibilities of this new force were five in number, in the following order of importance :

Firstly, the observation and prompt reporting of information. Although much of the countryside was very thinly inhabited, from dusk till dawn there must be no spot in it that was not under the watchful eye of the local L.D.V. The observation posts were chosen, and each platoon commander was instructed to make the necessary arrangements to man those that came into his district. Any untoward incident must be notified to the police immediately, either by runner or telephone, and this was to be considered the most important duty. Indeed, fire-eaters were told emphatically that no private war must be started with enemy parachutists until a message had first been sent to the local police, giving the number, time, and place of their arrival.

Secondly, the delay and obstruction of the enemy by every possible means. In the beginning the means would be weak, but a promise was given that they would be strengthened as soon as possible.

Thirdly, in certain districts the protection of specific points such as factories, telephone exchanges, railway stations, and the like.

Fourthly, a continuous check on subversive activities, all members of the L.D.V. to guard their own tongues, and to listen to those of their neighbours.

And, fifthly, a close co-operation at all times with the Civil Defence services.

Usually there was some discussion of the question or discipline and its maintenance throughout the force, and generally it was agreed that while discipline was necessary, in a voluntary unpaid force such as the L.D.V., it could be maintained only if it was based on two things : firstly, on the leadership and personality of its officers ; and secondly, on an L.D.V. spirit.

The spirit of the L.D.V. was already in being as evinced by the way in which all sorts and conditions of men had hurried to enrol in it. However, on enrolment each volunteer had undertaken certain responsibilities, one of the most essential being to submit himself to a form of military discipline, without which no body of men could hope to compete with a professional enemy. Otherwise he had enrolled either under false pretences or misapprehension, was of no value, and better out of the L.D.V. Therefore, it would be the leaders' duty to make that point clear when and where it might be necessary. Even so, L.D.V. discipline could not and must not depend for its efficiency on any form of penalty or punishment. Instead, it must be based on intelligent co-operation, self-sacrifice, fairness, and common sense. In short, the L.D.V. could be led, and must be led ; but it could not be driven, and there must be no attempt to drive it.

Another vexed question in those early days was that of transport—how were the men to travel to and from the observation posts ?—and the suggestion that either feet or bicycles would perform this brought disagreement and help from farmer members in every rural parish in Britain. They pointed out that most villages were in valleys, which meant that the O.P. would be at least two miles distant, and uphill all the way ; that most of the men would have done a long day's manual work, and would have to begin another the moment they finished their L.D.V. duty ; that the majority would be by no means youngsters, and that in farming they were considered much too valuable to waste their energies by walking. Also they stressed that the progress of modern war and modern farming, two things that had always used similar transport, emphasized the advantage. and indeed the necessity for mechanical transport. The farmers said this loud and clear, and some, thanks be, went so far as to shout their views on this subject in everybody's ear.

They might be but N.C.O.'s in the L.D.V., but when it came to dealing with country workmen and rural transport they considered themselves the superior of any and every army officer. Having been told that no transport was available, they asked for petrol to drive their own cars. Being refused this, they demanded coupons, in order that they might buy the petrol out of their own pockets. And when even this privilege was denied them they guaranteed to haul the men at their own expense until such time as the authorities learned sense.

Here in all fairness it must be stated that before many weeks had passed the authorities did issue the necessary petrol coupons and arrange to pay for the petrol used on L.D.V. duty, but in the beginning the whole of the cost of this transport was borne by the private motorist in country districts.

No doubt in years to come critics will pour scorn on these early arrangements and decisions, but to their credit must be stated two things. Firstly, they quickly put into active service a large force of part-time soldiers of sorts, which by its very existence may have helped to prevent an invasion of this country during those dangerous days of summer, 1940. Secondly, they illustrated once again the British genius for compromise.

CHAPTER 2

Watch and Ward

Having received its preliminary instructions, the L.D.V. immediately proceeded to institute a night watch over all Britain. About a dozen rifles and uniforms per platoon came to hand during the first week, and these caused many arguments and jealousies.

The non-Service members could not understand the extraordinary insistence on the part of the ex-Service men upon obtaining a uniform to fit.

" What does a uniform matter ? " they argued. " What we want is a rifle apiece, and lashings of ammunition."

But neither rifles, ammunition, nor uniforms were available in sufficient numbers for each man to have his own, and so recriminations and quarrels resulted, often to the despair of some well-meaning section leader, who did not appreciate two essential things : firstly, that every member of the L.D.V. was a little boy who would not be happy until he had his own pop-gun ; and secondly, that every ex-Service man was a Beau Brummel when it came to the question of the fit of his uniform.

As a matter of interest, two years of L.D.V. and Home Guard administration in a rural district have taught me that the majority of its country members have small feet, large heads, and are rather under average in height ; also that middle age usually boasts a middle of some rotundity. I mention that because for a long time the customary issue was boots sizes ten to eleven, hats and steel helmets size six and five-eighths, and uniforms for men six feet high and of lamp-post silhouette.

However, in the beginning the uniforms were but khaki

denim overalls. In most cases these, even when worn over a civilian suit, draped about two and a half times around and over their wearers. Consequently when an ex-Service man found a uniform that more or less fitted, did he obey orders and return it to store ready for the next night's squad ? No, he carefully took it home, until the original dozen uniforms was whittled down to about three that had evidently been made for slim Goliaths ; whereupon the next O.P. squad mutinied until the long-suffering section leader motored round the district from house to house in search of lost clothing.

But in spite of these troubles and many others the watch was kept, and each night on every hilltop in Britain four slovenly clad soldiers of sorts did duty from dusk till dawn. Usually a farmer member provided an old shepherd's hut on wheels for shelter, and hauled it by tractor or horses to the selected position. Members with cars provided transport for the other three in their squad, and the roster worked out at about one night's duty for each man per week.

In order to give a true picture of the way in which the L.D.V. carried out its early work and training I shall have to tell many tales out of school ; so the victims of my perfidy shall be the Sedgebury Wallop Platoon, or, to give them their official title, Number Seven Platoon, B Company, of the Eleventh Battalion of the Wessex L.D.V., later of the Wessex Home Guard. For safety's sake I hasten to state that, to the best of my knowledge and belief, Sedgebury Wallop does not exist, and that there never has been a Wessex Battalion of either L.D.V. or Home Guard. But for my purpose Sedgebury Wallop is a mythical but typical South Country village that nestles under the downs as though it had grown there, and the members of its platoon are typical countrymen, whose counterparts can be found in every rural platoon in Britain. Here is how they went on duty in May 1940.

The squad consisted of Section Leader Pocock, and

Volunteers Yates, Goodridge, and Bridle. In village language it was made up of Farmer Pocock, Shep Yates, Carter Goodridge, and Lightnin' Bridle; or, in order of merit, two good men, one fairish, and t'other a trifle wanting.

No one in Sedgebury Wallop ever questioned Walter Pocock's ability to make a good showing at anything to which he set his hand; Yates, a man with a national reputation as a shepherd and an old soldier, commanded every one's respect; Goodridge was a fair carter and a quiet man whom no one could dislike; while Bridle's nickname denoted that as a baker's roundsman and in every other activity this gangling lad of seventeen shone only by reason of his lack of speed. But, as Walter Pocock had argued with his colleagues, " 'Tis silly to put all good men or all fools together; we must mix 'em up."

This was the first taste of soldiering for three members of the squad, so it had been arranged that their change from civilian attire to uniform should take place in the privacy of the farmer's harness-room, out of sight of the interested gaze of, as he put it, " ten thousand kids and the whole blasted village." In these days such shyness may seem rather far-fetched, but then it was very real. Moreover, in the early days few people took the L.D.V. seriously, which was why the farmer's car was parked in the horse-yard just outside the harness-room door, in order that the squad might obtain a flying start into the lane, and so prevent undue ribaldry from the crowd of watchers.

In the seclusion of the harness-room each member of the squad sorted over the twelve denim uniforms in hope of finding one to fit, but with varying success. Shepherd Yates was the only really lucky man. When he had slipped his medal ribbons into his khaki blouse he not only looked a soldier, but felt ready to prove it. But Goodridge and Lightnin' could do no better than battle-dress that enveloped them, while Walter Pocock had to be content with a blouse and a cap, there being no pair of trousers large enough to contain his ample belly and posterior.

True, he was not unduly worried over this deficiency, being of the opinion that uniform didn't matter a hoot, but the cap moved him to bad language. Again, there was nothing large enough, and so a six and three-eighths size cap had to be perched precariously on a seven and one-quarter size cranium, most of which was bald and shiny.

" Blast the thing," he exclaimed wrathfully. " It won't stay put for one minute. Put it on back and front, and in two seconds it's drifted sideways. Bloody ridiculous."

" You wants to clamp 'er down firm awver one eyebrow, maister," was his shepherd's advice. " Gi'e the gels a treat like. See—Lightnin's got the daps ov it."

This was true. Lightnin' might be slow, and his uniform at least five sizes too large for him, the trousers falling like a concertina round his ankles ; but on his small head, or rather resting on his right ear, an army cap sat in most jaunty fashion.

" God Almighty ! " muttered Walter at this shameful sight, and turned for relief to look at Carter Goodridge. That patient man, now fully clothed in uniform and looking the picture of misery, was staring gloomily at the strange headgear in his gnarled hands.

" Cheer up, Carter," said Walter. " Next time I'll have a looking-glass in here for you."

Into the dressing-room of this untried male chorus now came Tom Butler, the miller, an ex-soldier section leader, who burst into hoots of laughter at the sights he found there.

" Sorry, chaps, and all that," he apologized, wiping his eyes, " but it really is a bit much. Shep's fit for church parade, and possibly Carter and Lightnin' would pass on active service, which, of course, this is, but Walter—help ! You'd be crimed in Ally Sloper's army. Damn it, you'd be shot at dawn. Where on earth are your trousers ? "

" Nowhere," growled his friend. " And I can do without 'em, Tom, but these blasted hats are the limit."

" You never spoke a truer word, Walter. Say, got everything ? Rifles, ammo, and gas-masks ? Right, then ; let' see the squad fall in."

Shamefacedly three of the four stood in line with the shepherd. Tom grinned at them, and then suddenly said, " Squad ! Shun ! Slope ARMS ! "

The shepherd's rifle went up to his shoulder like clockwork, and after many struggles the other three eventually found a similar resting-place.

" My God ! " murmured Tom to himself, but, seeing that any further jesting would be unfair, he said aloud, " That's the stuff, chaps. There's no doubt about it— Hitler don't know what he's up against. Away you go, and good luck."

The squad piled into the car, and as the vehicle turned into the lane the crowd outside cheered lustily, one wag yelling with glee, " Thank God we got a navy."

But while every one in Britain echoed that sentiment at all times, the fact remains that a few minutes afterwards Walter Pocock's car was parked in a chalk-pit on Ludcombe Down where some thorn-bushes gave good cover to both it and the shepherd's hut that had been hauled into position earlier in the day, and near by four armed men kept watch on the surrounding countryside.

Soon afterwards another car crept slowly up the farm road, and came to a halt under a spreading beech-tree perhaps a quarter of a mile distant from the O.P. From it emerged Sir Robert Enfield in the uniform of his old regiment, a relic of the previous war. He was wearing to seventy, but he strode across the short turf like a man forty years younger.

" I 'low we best try to come to attention, zur, when wold Bobby do arrive," was Shep's comment, as the platoon

commander approached. " It'll plaze the wold chap
tremendous."

They did their best, and were duly complimented. Their
officer stayed chatting with them for a quarter of an hour,
during which he managed to depress Walter Pocock still
further.

" Ah, I see you have the hut well hidden, Pocock.
Capital. But next time I think you would be well advised
to leave your car on the road. Otherwise you'll soon make
a track on the turf that will be visible from the air, and so
give away the position of this O.P. That's right, isn't it,
Yates ? "

Shep, torn between the habit of obedience to an officer,
the knowledge that the criticism was sound, and the respect
due to his employer, was forced to agree. Whereupon the
remainder of the conversation was between two old soldiers,
the three raw recruits listening respectfully.

Shortly after Sir Robert's departure Walter Pocock
looked at his watch to find that it was a few minutes after
eleven.

" Time to split up," he remarked. " Shep, you and
Goodridge turn in till I call you just after two. Bridle and
I'll take the first watch."

But Bridle soon proved a broken reed. He was only just
seventeen, and he could not keep awake ; so soon after
midnight Walter told him to take a snooze in his car, as
there were only two camp-beds in the hut.

" Chap's only a kid, and not a very bright one at that,"
he muttered, as he resumed his watch over the countryside.
" Middle age is tougher than half-grown boys."

But he soon decided that toughness, even his middle-
aged toughness, was not sufficient qualification for this new
job that war had thrust upon him. At this soldiering
business he was so lamentably inefficient, so hopelessly a
tyro, a rôle that never had and even now did not suit him.

The memory of his awkward ignorance when Tom Butler had jokingly ordered the squad to slope arms was not a pleasant one. How the hell had Shep got his rifle on to his shoulder? Alone on the downs at midnight Walter Pocock endeavoured to find out. He stood at attention with his rifle by his side, and tried various methods, but with no satisfactory result. True, he did get the rifle on to his shoulder, but somehow he knew that the method he used was all wrong.

" Yet I've been used to guns all my life," he remarked to the rising moon. " I can shoot with this damn thing better than most folk, certainly better than Tom, and probably better than Shep. But this tin soldier drill business I know nothing about. Ah, well, it'll be the shooting that'll matter most."

With this satisfying thought in his mind he tucked the rifle under his arm as though it was his twelve-bore shot-gun, and surveyed the moonlit scene before him.

Every inch of the country for miles around was as familiar to him as the palm of his right hand. He had farmed a good deal of it, and hunted and shot over every field. Away to his right lay the black mass of Ludcombe Wood, scene of cubbing mornings, pheasant shoots, courting rambles, and pleasant family picnics. Below him on the left the fields of the Manor Farm stretched in gentle swoops down to the valley meadows on either side of the river Brill. A shaft of moonshine suddenly picked out a cathedral spire some seven miles distant, and even as he looked upon its beauty and wondered whether some day it might not be used by the enemy as a bombing target, it disappeared once again into the silver night. An unseen train clanged through the valley below, a hare pottered quietly across the down not fifty yards away, and a snore from the sleeping Lightnin' made the amateur sentinel turn his head.

He stamped his feet, for it was cold, and the hare quickened

its pace immediately. It was cold, and the sooner the
authorities issued overcoats to the L.D.V. the better. Not
that he needed one, for his mackintosh was a good one, but
the men, at any rate many of them, would need a warm
coat for this job. It never occurred to him for one moment
that the only part of his attire and equipment that marked
him as a soldier was his cap, which by now sat athwart his
bald head in truly Napoleonic fashion.

The whole business was absurd, fantastic. That he,
Walter Pocock, should be up on Ludcombe Down in the
middle of the night waiting for, watching for, almost hoping
for, the enemy to appear. Bah ! The enemy would never
appear. England had not been invaded since William the
Conqueror, and would never be invaded in his, Walter
Pocock's, lifetime. He tried to remember the dates of the
Norman kings, but failed after William Rufus.

" Who was shot by a bow and arrow in the New Forest,"
he informed the night. " Brr ! It is cold."

He stamped his feet again, and discovered a curious
satisfaction in the feel of the solid earth beneath his feet.
This little bit of England, Manor Farm, Sedgebury Wallop,
was his, anyway. He had worked hard to earn the money
to buy it, and no one could ever take it from him now. Or
could they ? What good was either property or money now ?
What good was anything or what good could be anywhere
until Hitler and his ideas had been exterminated ? Well,
he would guard this, his own bit of England, in spite of
anything and everybody.

Then it suddenly occurred to him that he was not merely
guarding his own little bit of property, but that he, a man
who valued individualism and scorned all crowds, was now
part and parcel of a volunteer force that had undertaken
to guard, not personal property, but national property,
with no thought of payment for services rendered. Which
was absurd for Walter Pocock, a man who always had his

eye to the main chance, and very definitely a man who should have had more sense at fifty-five than to stand on the downs in the middle of the night just to catch a cold.

Yes, that might be silly, and people might and probably would laugh at him as an old fool now trying to play at soldiers, both of which he could bear while the necessity remained. But what he could not bear was the thought that of all the men who were playing at soldiers that night he was probably the most inefficient. He decided that he would take steps to learn this new job, even drill—yes, damn it, even saluting—as soon as possible. Tom Butler was an old soldier, and Tom was his friend. Right! Tom should teach him his drill, so that he would no longer feel quite such a fool, the biggest fool in the L.D.V. Ah, what was that?

His foxhunter's eye had caught the suspicion of a movement on the far side of the down. He watched it carefully. A long, low shape moved towards him on the slope, stopping every few moments for reconnaissance.

The sentinel suddenly relaxed his poise, and chuckled. The fox came right up to within twenty yards, and then sat staring at this strange night-watcher, who would have been quite content to admire his new companion indefinitely. But his army cap betrayed him. Suddenly it slipped off his bald head, and the fox vanished in the moonlight at an easy lope, occasionally looking behind him.

" Pass, friend. All's well," muttered the sentry, as he stooped to retrieve his headgear.

Just before 2 A.M. he waked Lightnin', and shortly afterwards he and that yawning youth changed places with their two companions. For the next three hours the watch was under the able command of Shep, while the snores of youth and middle age dominated the dark interior of the shepherd's hut. Then all four watched the dawn until full daylight ordained that they should drive down the hill to take up their civil duties.

The following evening another squad left the harness-room after much grumbling concerning the ill-fitting uniforms provided.

" It beats me," remarked Walter to Tom Butler. " These old soldiers worry over clothes worse than a woman. Who wants a blooming uniform anyway ? I don't."

" Of course you don't, Walter, for the simple reason that you've never worn one. Look, you're doin' fine, but you've got a hell of a lot to learn about this job. Uniform's important."

" May be, but must it fit like a fashion-plate before an old soldier'll stand on Ludcombe Down in it all night ? "

" No, but he'll feel a lot happier and be a much better watcher if it does fit. Walter, this job has to be done by the men available, and it's our job to keep 'em happy. Otherwise the job won't get done properly."

" Keep 'em happy ? Damn it ! I'm worryin' over 'em so much that I'm neglecting my own business. I've cleared out the harness-room for 'em, hauled a hut up there for 'em to sleep in, and provided transport. What the hell else ought I to do ? "

" Something quite as important as anything you have done. Study their pride. Without pride no soldier's worth a damn."

" Pride in what ? Uniform and a lot of fal-lals ? Spicer asked me the other day how long it would be before we had an issue of regimental cap badges. How in hell can cap badges help to tackle the job we've been asked to do ? "

" They can and all, and before very long you'll know why. But that isn't as important as rifles. We do want a rifle for every man."

" I'll agree there, Tom. If Jerry came over here now we'd be a fat lot of use with fifty men and twelve rifles."

" Yes, but a rifle per man is important even if Jerry never comes. A soldier wants his own rifle, to take it home, and clean it, and love it like his wife. Every soldier just hates to think of anyone touching his rifle. Walter, you've got a lot to learn."

"All right, and I'll learn it. But first I want to learn something more useful than choosing a uniform to fit. I don't like being at the bottom of the class, Tom. Night duty I can manage, uniform or no uniform, but some fine day there'll be how d'you do in public, and then I'll be sunk. I can shoot with a rifle, but I don't know how to handle the bally thing according to your standards. So you, little man, shall now have the fun of your life teaching me the rudiments of drill."

"Walter, you're coming on. I wanted to suggest that, but hardly knew how you'd take it. But you ain't the only rooky, not by no means. There's Lightnin', Goodridge, Smith, Kendle—oh, a round dozen or more. We don't want much drill in the L.D.V., but we do want to know how to get out of the way of our own feet. Right, we'll start a recruits' squad, and drill evenings on the green."

"Not for a thousand pounds, no, never, Tom. There's a limit. I'll clear out the big barn, and you can do your damnedest in private. But I'll see you and the L.D.V. in Hades before I'll be laughed at in public."

Tom Butler chuckled. "And this," he murmured happily, "was the man who only a few moments ago said that pride didn't matter. Walter, you're learning fast. Your pride won't let you learn your drill in public. Right, I'll respect that pride, and we'll drill in your barn. In return you will think twice before you bark at an old soldier who takes pride in his uniform, or who wants cap badges."

"All right, Tom ; but look, you must ride me hardest. Otherwise t'others won't play. Got it ? "

Tom Butler nodded happily. "Walt, as I said before, you're learning fast."

The first parade of the awkward squad took place two

nights later, when nine shamefaced men met Tom Butler in the big barn of the Manor Farm. They were in civilian clothes, but each carried a long rifle of the P.14 type, and most of them were leaning on this weapon for support. The large window was open for light as it was too high up for any onlooker, but the doors were closed for privacy.

" Right ! " said Tom. " We'll get going. Now look, chaps, you're here because you want to learn a bit about your new job, and I'm here to help. What I say on parade means nothing off parade, so no one need take offence at anything I say. Agreed ? "

The squad nodded. Whereupon the man they knew as Tom Butler the miller suddenly changed into a drill sergeant.

" Right ! Fall in. Lumme, you don't know how to. Pocock, you stand here. That's it. Now then, you others get in line with him."

He surveyed the result, and shook his head.

" In line with Pocock I said. Not like a zig-zag path. Damn it, imagine you're drivin' partridges. Cover off from the right."

This done more or less, Tom manhandled each man into the stand-easy position, and then explained the method by which they would come to attention at the word of command. After ten minutes' practice they could do this to his satisfaction, so he next proceeded to initiate them into the mysteries of sloping arms and other simple drill movements, his running commentary surprising everybody, including himself.

" For pity's sake get hold of your rifles. Pocock, it won't bite you, man. Cuddle the damn' thing as though it were your best girl. Now then, slope arms by numbers. One, two, three."

The squad obeyed.

" Holy suffering Michael ! I wish you could see yourselves. And don't shuffle. Stand still, can't you ? Bad as it is, for God's sake, hold it."

In pain and grief the squad did their best to hold it, while Tom explained the movements and commands for ordering arms. The result was calamitous. Lightnin' somehow managed to order his rifle on his left side ; Pocock dropped his with a clatter on the floor ; and the others brought theirs down to earth with an irregular and noisy tattoo.

" It beats cock-fighting," murmured Tom aloud. " One butter-fingers at the end, seven men pitching hurdles, and Lightnin' working out a new drill on his own. Stand still, Pocock."

Walter stood still and silent, although the back of his huge neck and his countenance were now a dull crimson.

" The guardsman who dropped it, I don't think," came from his instructor. " All right. I'll use his rifle for a while. Squad ! Stand-at—EASE."

" H'm, not so bad. Easy ! Now then—watch me."

They watched in admiration while the rifle moved in Tom's hands like easy clockwork. In a few moments he handed it back to the culprit who had dropped it with the words, " Now then, tuck that belly out of the way, and try to think what you're doing."

For an hour and a half he wrought with them faithfully, eventually bringing some semblance of order out of the original chaos, and finally dismissing them with the compliment that they had done well and that in his view the worst was over.

" And now," he beamed at them, " seeing that we've knocked off the rough edges we'll all go down to the Wheat-sheaf, and I'll buy the drinks. Come along."

But the squad would not permit this. Strange to say the recruits were sincerely grateful to their instructor, and vowed that the drinks were on them.

CHAPTER 3

Beginners' Luck

THE evacuation from Dunkirk with all that it implied shocked the whole British nation. People who had honestly thought that by some special dispensation Britain was sacrosanct from invasion or even defeat now abandoned their " it can't happen here " belief. Indeed, the general public was suddenly so frightened and worried that a portion of it began to respect the L.D.V. as men who were not just playing at soldiers, but as men who were giving up time, money, and all sorts of things in order to become more proficient.

In fairness the point about money must be made. Later on arrangements were made whereby moneys expended by members of the L.D.V. for transport and other necessaries were refunded, but in the early days there was not one platoon commander or section leader who did not dip his hand into his pocket every week on behalf of the force.

Time, too, is money, and every member gave up time, much time to the early training. Where the platoon commander realized his responsibilities, he chose the right section leaders and organized the training. In cases, and there were some, where he considered it his duty to be only a figurehead, having taken the position far more in order to establish his social superiority than to make his platoon efficient, his section leaders and his men forced his hand, and got some useful training going.

The great difficulty was the paucity of arms and equipment, and for many weeks the majority of platoons had but twelve rifles and half a dozen shot-guns for perhaps a hundred men. This state of things was bad for the morale of the force, and members of it were often heard to wish that recruiting had been controlled to match the supply of equipment. Indeed, there was no doubt that an L.D.V. without his own rifle was a disgruntled man.

Still, most volunteers realized that equipment did not grow in a night as the force had done, and also that an enormous amount had been lost in France. Also that the rescued army must have first call on new arms and equipment; that the second must be granted to the L.D.V. in the south-east corner of England where the first bump would most likely come; and that the remainder must wait their turn and man their O.P.'s as best they could with the materials available.

Immediately after Dunkirk the L.D.V. was given another job in addition to their original one of watch and ward. This was the institution of a frequent check on road traffic. There was no regular day in the week for this, but it might be ordered at short notice on any evening, sometimes because certain cars and their occupants were being hunted.

Most car drivers took this dusk till dawn inquisition good-humouredly, as a necessary evil of the times; but few realized the risk they ran when arriving at an L.D.V. road block, or that those in charge were armed with ball ammunition. For instance, a man driving XYZ 372 was unaware that XYZ 572 was suspect, and that half a dozen stalwart L.D.V. were itching for a chance to shoot.

At this time weary, half-clad soldiers from France were passing through the railway stations night and day, and rumours of spies abounded. Everybody felt that at any moment the news of invasion would come, and suspense ruled the whole country. Even so there were people who scoffed at the very idea of invasion, and who ridiculed the newly formed L.D.V. and its amateurish attempts to do soldiers' work. Some of these tried to have fun with these volunteers; some who knew no better and some who should have known much better. But after one or two regrettable incidents the public realized that these men were doing a tiring job for no pay, and also that it was safest to obey their requests without argument.

The man who refused to show his identity card on the grounds that he had " shown the damn' thing twenty times in the last thirty miles " and who swore at those who now demanded it, found his car key abstracted, his car pushed to the side of the road, and his person held until the civil police took over and gave him the necessary reprimand. The man who drove on when challenged, thinking " these yokels won't dare to shoot," was shot at and usually hit. Again Sedgebury Wallop shall provide the examples.

Owing to some one falling sick at the last moment, Lightnin', of all people, was inspecting identity cards at the village cross-roads one evening, a duty which he performed with his rifle slung across his back.

" And if anyone poked a revolver at the fool," remarked a motorist in a hotel bar who had just suffered Lightnin's methods, " he'd be dead long before he could get at his rifle. Why doesn't some one teach these chaps the rudiments of their job ? "

A young officer who heard this remark decided to have fun with Lightnin' on his drive back to his billet. When asked for his identity card he pulled out his revolver and pointed it at the inquisitor.

" Hi, Shep. Shoot," yelled Lightnin'. And from the comfortable perch of a chair in a secluded porch Shep sent a bullet through the culprit's backside on the instant.

On another evening half an hour after turn-out time, Candy Taylor, the local drunkard, weaved unsteadily up the village street towards the cross-roads. When halted and asked for his identity card he beamed at Sergeant Butler and his men, and said, " Shertainly, Maister Butler, shertainly. I keeps 'im cosy in me wes—in me wuscat, in me . . ."

The effort of fumbling into the deep recesses of his long-sleeved corduroy waistcoat was too much for Candy's equilibrium, and down he fell on to the road.

" Come on, get up, you old soak," said Tom, but Candy never moved, and a stertorous snore was his only answer.

" He's out, out for the count," chuckled Tom. " Ah, well, it's a warm night, so he can sleep it off out of doors. Come on, Spicer, give us a hand."

Carefully they lifted the unconscious Candy and deposited him on the bank at the side of the road.

An hour later, when the traffic had thinned almost to nothing, Tom and Walter were snatching a well-earned forty winks in a car, leaving the command of the road block in the capable hands of Shep Yates, now a full-blown corporal. Presently a car approached the block, and came to a halt at the bidding of a waved red lamp.

" What the devil is it now ? " came in disgruntled tones from the driver.

" Jist wants to see yer identity card, maister," came from Shep.

This request in broad dialect told the driver of the car that his questioner was a yokel, so he decided to bluff his way through.

" No, I'm damned if I'll show it," he retorted. " I've shown the thing half a dozen times in the last twenty miles. It's ridiculous."

" Reedicklus er no, you'd baste show 'er," advised Shep.

" Like hell I will. You chaps are only grown-up Boy Scouts. You enjoy playing at soldiers just like a lot of kids. I'm not showing my card again, and I'm driving on. See ? "

" I 'low I shouldn't goo fer to do that, maister," advised Shep. " You zee, zummat's up to-night. We don't know wot, but any feller wot do drive on wi'out permission we be shootin'."

C

" Pooh ! " scoffed the motorist. " Shoot me ? More than you dare do."

" Ah," said Shep with evident relish. " That's wot 'ee thought," and he jerked his thumb to Candy's apparently dead body on the bank by the side of the road.

Whereat a badly frightened motorist produced his identity card in a hurry, and would have produced much money to avoid a similar fate.

" Good God ! " he muttered as he drove away. " Fancy laying their victims out on the bank like rabbits at the end of a day's shoot. These fellows are bloody Nazis. Something ought to be done about it."

During that precarious post-Dunkirk period perhaps a dozen people were shot by the L.D.V. in Britain, which encouraged the others to such good purpose that no further occasion to fire was forthcoming after the first week or two.

But that they were amateurs there was no disputing. They did their best to behave as soldiers at the beginning of each night's traffic check, but as soon as darkness came they unashamedly behaved as what they were and what they were intended to be—useful bandits. They had worked hard at their civil jobs all day, and would have to do so on the morrow with only an uncomfortable nap of three hours in the back of a car to refresh them. So after dark they saved themselves as much fatigue as possible. They borrowed chairs from the houses near by, and sat on them, which was, according to the ex-Service man, devilish near high treason. But, in spite of this unsoldierly proceeding, every car was brought to a halt for examination.

Their orders were definite, but the manner in which those same orders were carried out was left to their own gumption. Naturally they learned much from experience. For example, one evening Tom Butler stopped a ten-horse Austin car, green in colour, registration CMR 864. The driver, a young officer, felt in his coat pocket, and then said,

" Damn ! I've been playing tennis this afternoon, and left my pass in my tunic when I changed into flannels. Well, what's the penalty ? "

" I'm afraid you cannot pass, sir. Unless you can get some one to vouch for you."

" And if I cannot, what then ? Shot at dawn ? "

" Oh no, sir. We shall just hold you up and ring the police. It's their job to decide whether you can pass or not."

" And how long before the police arrive on the scene ? "

" May be an hour, sir. Just depends whether anyone is free at the station."

" But, look here, my wife and I want to get home. And they'll rag me unmercifully in the mess. Isn't there any other way out ? "

" Well, sir, can you tell me anything that may enable me to verify your identity ? "

" Shouldn't think so, but we'll try. Look here, my name is Rogers, Captain Rogers. I'm stationed at Linchbury." And he gave his company and the telephone number of its orderly room.

" Right, sir. Just drive round the corner, and we'll ring up."

The officer did so, stood by the telephone box while Tom got the right number, and then listened to one-half of the following conversation :

" That Linchbury 271 ? "

" Yes, sir. Pioneers, 105 Company."

" Wessex L.D.V. here. Can I speak to Captain Rogers ? "

" Captain Rogers is out, sir. Driven to Yarborough Tennis Club, I think. Is there anything I can do ? "

" Yes, it's a question of identity. Your Captain Rogers is about five feet seven, thick-set, with fair hair ? "

" Oh no, sir. Our Captain Rogers is over six feet, thin, with black hair."

" H'm ! The officer here is driving an eight-horse

Morris saloon, painted red, CMW 276. You couldn't let me know what your Captain Rogers drives, I suppose ? "

" Oh yes, sir. He drives an Austin Ten, green saloon, CMR 864. I'm afraid you've got the wrong man, sir."

" Right. Thank you very much. Good-bye."

Tom turned to the tall, dark officer, who was now grinning happily, and said, " Right, sir. It seems good enough. Anyway, I'll take a chance on it. Sorry to have hung you up like this."

" Not at all. I'm sorry to have given you all this trouble. Moreover, I'd like to say two things—first, to compliment the L.D.V. on the tactful and sensible way you tackled this job, and second, that if you had let me pass without checking up like this I should have reported you. Good-night."

" And that bloke," remarked Tom, when he told the tale to Walter Pocock, " was a gentleman."

" Which is a damn' sight more than the Staff wallah poor old Goodridge stopped the other night," growled the other.

" Oh, what happened ? "

" Well, you know how that denim uniform drapes on old Goodridge. This bloke gave up his pass all right, and then said, ' So that's the uniform they've issued to you fellows. My God, you look like nothing on earth.' However, I was coming across to help Goodridge, and heard it, so I cut in with, ' Your uniform may fit, sir, but your manners don't. Of all people you should be the last to sneer at a volunteer in the L.D.V.' "

" Walter, you didn't ! You were fair askin' for trouble. What on earth did he say ? "

" Spluttered that he would report me for insolence, so I gave him my name and the number of my platoon, and advised him to drive on. Which he did. And I'll lay you fifty to one he don't report anything."

" He won't. But isn't it tragic that one pig in five hundred can and does give the general public a totally wrong impression of the average army officer? Still, there's one good thing shows out of that incident, Walter."

" Oh, what ? "

" Merely that the man who sneered at pride is now very proud of the L.D.V., and jumps to defend it."

" Rubbish ! But, look here, Tom, we've so much of this traffic duty now that sometimes it has to be done by men who cannot be expected to hold up an officer without a pass in the same way that you did it. Such a man might bluster his way through, and then report us. We should have our orders in writing."

They put this up to their C.O. at the next opportunity. He immediately saw the wisdom of it, and issued type-written instructions for traffic checking, giving a list of the necessary passes required by all ranks in the Services, and a definite order that none was to be allowed to pass unless in possession of the correct document.

A few days later Walter stopped a car about midnight, and the army officer who was driving it produced his pass. Walter studied it by the light of his torch, to find that although it was evidently an official document, it was very different from the usual one carried by army officers.

" I'm sorry, sir," he said, " but I cannot pass you on this. It appears to be in order, but it is not the one I must see."

" Ah, you want so and so," mentioning the letter and number of the pass Walter had expected. " Well, this one supersedes that. It is granted only to officers above a certain rank. It enables me to go anywhere in Britain."

" Possibly, sir, but with the exception of this road block. To get by here you must produce so and so."

" Which just proves, my man, that you don't know your job."

" Very true, sir. I'm an amateur all right. Even so, you cannot pass."

" And how will you stop me ? "

Walter stooped swiftly and abstracted the ignition key of the car, at the same time calling for Shep and Lightnin'. These worthies now stood in front of the car with their rifles at the ready.

" H'm ! I see. You seem very sure of yourself, my man."

" Not at all, sir. Just obeying orders."

" Got those orders in writing ? "

" Yes, sir. Here they are. You will note that army officers are not to be passed unless in possession of a pass lettered and numbered very differently from yours."

" H'm ! Who is your C.O. ? "

" Sir Robert Enfield, sir."

" Good God ! I'm going to stay with him, man."

" Then if you will wait here, sir, I will ring him up. We'll just push your car off the fairway."

" And who," demanded the Brigadier, after his friend had rescued him, " is your stalwart section leader, Bobby ? He'd have shot me for tuppence."

" Shouldn't wonder. Sidney, you want to be careful with the L.D.V. But he's a local farmer, and a tower of strength. Whenever I see his hind-end blocking the village street I feel that Britain's still safe."

But it was when Australia met the L.D.V. that their status was most aptly described. One evening the last bus from Yarborough decanted an Australian private, who evidently had imbibed more beer than was good for him. He did not know where he was and said so, mourning that he wanted to go to Luxford Camp. As this place was nearly twenty miles distant from Sedgebury Wallop, Tom Butler advised him to sleep it off on a seat by the churchyard wall, informing him that before long the L.D.V. would stop a car going his way, and procure him a lift.

No such car came along for an hour or so, and then the sleeper awoke. He wobbled unsteadily through the night ;

and, as Tom was examining a driver's pass on the offside of a car, its near door, by the driver's wife, opened, and a drunken voice said, " Arresh that man. Arresh him, I tell you. He'sh a bloody spy."

The driver said, " Look here, I don't mind you fellows doing your job, but I do object to that."

" So do I," said Tom, and called two men, who shouldered the offender on to the pavement. The car drove away, and Tom then warned his critic to stay put on the pavement lest worse befall him.

" Not at all. Not at all. You doh know your job, so I'm going to teach it to you. I'm an exhperst."

" You may be, sonny, but we can do without your help. You stay on the pavement until we get a lift for you."

For the best part of an hour he annoyed them, until Tom could stand the nuisance no longer.

" You butt in again, sonny, and we'll run you in," he warned.

" Run me in. Run in an Aushstraliansh soldier. More'n you daresh do. Leave me alone, an' I'll inshtruct you free."

" All right. You watch us try."

Tom sent Spicer to wake up the other half of the squad, who were taking a well-earned nap in his and Walter Pocock's car. When these reinforcements arrived he warned the trouble once again.

" Now look, sonny. One more break from you, and you're for it, certain, so watch your step."

" Rubbish ! You can't do without me. You doh know your job. Thash why I'm here."

He interfered again when the next car came along, so Tom immediately ran him up against the wall at the point of the bayonet, whereupon all resistance collapsed.

" An' what do we do with the fathead now ? If we run him in according to instructions it means ringing up the police, and they'll jug him. And then his C.O.'ll come down, and there'll be an inquiry and a hoo-ha of all sorts. 'Tain't worth it. Tell you what, Walter. Spicer and I'll frog-march him out of the village. You walk behind in case of trouble. When we get him on the road we'll give him a shove towards Yarborough. He's too full to find his way back. You others carry on here."

They made it so, but after the procession had gone some two hundred yards the prisoner brought himself and his two guards down in a clatter on the tarred road, with the result that Spicer put his thumb out.

" And now we are mad," muttered Tom, grasping the prisoner in no gentle fashion. " Come on, you."

At this moment a car pulled up, and an officer got out.

" What's all this ? " he inquired.

" Nothing much, sir," said Tom. " Bit of trouble with some one who has had a drop too much. He's been annoying us for hours, so we were running him out of town, so to speak."

" H'm ! Rather high-handed. You L.D.V. chaps can't take the law into your own hands like that."

" Jusht what I say," bellowed the prisoner. " I'm glad you've come, sir. They doh know their job, and I've been teaching them. It's shameful. Here I've come thousands of miles to fight for England, and I've been asshaulted by a lot of bloody amateurs."

This remark was so true, yet so funny, that both Walter and Tom collapsed into helpless laughter.

" It's no laughing matter," said the officer. " You have evidently grossly exceeded your duty."

" Jusht what I've been telling theesh cockies all the evening," agreed the prisoner. " Ineffishents, ineffishents, doh know their job, and exsheeds their duty. Asshaulted me."

At this moment a lorry rumbled up going towards Yarborough.

"It's the milk lorry, Walter. Stop her," yelled Tom.

Walter flagged the lorry with his torch, and when it halted, Tom said, "Good. Hang on to this twirp, Walter, while I fix it."

Then to the lorry-driver, "Bill, you're a friend in need. Do a job for me?"

"Certainly, Mr Butler."

"Right. Here's a half-crown. Take this lump o' trouble—it's quite harmless—and dump it in Yarborough outside the police-station. It's on your way. Come on, Walter," and with a jerk they hoisted the prisoner into the cab of the lorry, and slammed the door.

The lorry rumbled away, and the remainder of the players of this night farce surveyed each other on the moonlit stage. Spicer nursed his thumb in pain, Tom stood looking at the officer, while Walter picked up his rifle, and tried to stand to attention.

"And once again you have exceeded your duty. I shall report this," said the officer.

"Very good, sir," said Tom. "But we are all rather tired. You see, we've done a day's work before beginning this night duty, and that fellow had been annoying us past bearing. However, now he's gone, perhaps you will let me see your pass."

Fortunately the critic had forgotten it, and was forced to wait until a dispatch-rider arrived from Yarborough to identify him.

"Which," said Tom afterwards, "just shows that a Divine providence watches over the L.D.V."

"Or rather," growled Walter, "that drunken men speak the truth. For that's what we are—a lot of bloody amateurs. And it's a title that don't suit yours truly."

CHAPTER 4

Amateurs and Professionals

IN July 1940, by order of the Prime Minister, the official title of the new amateur force was changed from Local Defence Volunteers to Home Guard. At first, in spite of the love and respect that every member of the L.D.V. had for its author, this alteration was generally regretted, especially in rural districts, where the natural conservatism of the countryman rebelled against what he considered to be a needless change. Still, every one concerned was agreed that " Ower Winnie " had every right to call the tune, and that whatever he chose should be played by them to the best of their ability. So the section leaders distributed the new H.G. armlets, collected the now obsolete L.D.V. type, and carried on with the training. L.D.V., Home Guard, or Horse Guards, the job in hand remained the same as ever— to make themselves and their men as efficient as possible as quickly as possible.

Observation duty had now settled down to a regular feature of every man's everyday life ; while the evening and Sunday morning drill had turned what had been an unsoldierly rabble into a body of men who could obey simple orders without question, and who now yearned for less drill and more weapon training.

But weapons, uniforms, and all equipment were still in short supply, although each week a little of something or other did trickle in to each platoon. It might be half a dozen rifles, three greatcoats, four or five uniforms, or a few rifle-slings, and so on ; but whatever came to hand meant headaches and unpopularity for the section leaders. These unfortunates distributed the new equipment by the only sound method—to those men who turned up regularly on parade, in the matter of uniforms this choice being influenced by the necessity of finding a man to fit the suit. Yet no matter how many hours the section leader spent in trying to use the available equipment to the best advantage he was accused of both favouritism and negligence by the few in each platoon who did the least possible to help.

Of course, like every young thing the Home Guard had its teething troubles, but by this time the worst of these were over. In certain cases in the beginning it suffered from age, influence, and snobbery ; but these handicaps were being rapidly whittled down to a minimum. Also, it must be admitted that in the early days the old soldier members sometimes presented a difficult problem. They divided themselves into three distinct classes. Firstly, those who were not only willing to learn the new soldiering, but who were also willing to teach and help the tyros to learn the best of both old and new. Secondly, those who refused to take any rank or responsibility, and who were frankly scornful of the childish enthusiasm of the amateurs ; but who, in spite of everything, had decided that they would stay in this new and weird force until the need for it had passed. Thirdly, a minority who refused to parade, drill, or train, saying that they had finished with all that sort of thing twenty years before, and already knew all that was necessary.

As a civilian Home Guard I recognized the value of all three types, for I knew the enormous difference between an untried dog and one that had been shot over. Therefore, although as an enthusiastic amateur I deplored the attitude of the second class and resented that of the third, I was well aware of my and many others' limitations. These old soldiers had seen the slaughter at Vimy, on the Somme, and at Passchendaele ; I and thousands of others had seen none of such things. I might train and read and work hard at this new game, but what would happen when it had to be played in earnest? Frankly I did not know, and feared the worst of myself; but I did know that if certain crabbed old soldiers who now were annoying me intensely were either in front, alongside, or behind me, I should be obliged to play ball with them. So, no matter how awkward his attitude, I was always sorry when any of the old soldier members left the Home Guard, although sometimes I was forced to admit that they left it for its good.

For neither rank, fortune, nor camouflaged inefficiency can stand up for long to the discipline of life in a small community. There is one salutary lesson that every one who lives in an English village must learn, and the sooner he learns it the better—that while he may hide his light under a bushel, his shortcomings are known to all his neighbours. So the time soon came when the old soldier's "Ah, don't you worry about me not attending parades and lectures. When the balloon goes up you'll find me in the line alongside you," was countered with "But then we shan't want you, because you'll be a liability." At this the old soldier of every rank realized that his comrades were learning to use weapons that he had never handled and that he must either do the job properly or chuck it. To his credit be it said that in the main he chose the former alternative.

There were, too, a few volunteers of another type who failed to pull their weight. These were young civilians who were in reserved occupations and thus earning good wages. They considered that the Home Guard label was worth their while, but that they needed the whole of their leisure in order to spend and enjoy their earnings. Again the outspoken criticism of their neighbours worked the necessary cure.

Of the old soldier who gave of his best, first to the L.D.V. and subsequently to the Home Guard, I can write only with affection, gratitude, and respect. As section leader he was the guts of the average platoon. If his C.O. was an ex-officer and keen and energetic he worked for him like a Trojan. If that same officer happened to be indolent he prodded him at every touch and turn. If his platoon commander was a civilian, anxious about the efficiency of his platoon, but to whom even the simplest drill was a well-nigh insoluble problem, he taught him his job, covered up his mistakes, and backed him up at all times. He did the same for any civilian section leaders; he trained the men; he cheered them up when they were down; and he cut their combs with biting sarcasm when they were up a trifle too high. In short, he was the whole works, and it has been interesting and pleasing to note that as time went on more and more of this type of old soldier became platoon commanders or platoon officers.

Of all the men in the Home Guard it was this type of section leader who put the efficiency of the force before all else, and who was chiefly responsible for the selection of the right men to become N.C.O.'s. All other qualifications being equal, he naturally chose the man who boasted some previous military experience, but he never hesitated to recommend a civilian who had proved to him that he was the better man for the job.

Of course, even this Admirable Crichton had his prejudices, and the chief of these was his insistence that the weapon with which he was most familiar was the most essential. Thus the ex-musketry instructor told the novices that the rifle was the one thing that mattered, and that if they became proficient with this weapon, as they would do or he would know the reason why, they would be able to give Jerry what for. The ex-machine-gunner sneered at the rifle as an obsolete weapon, and demanded a machine-gun for every section of twenty men. The old artilleryman scoffed at both rifle and machine-gun as flimsy toys, and stressed

the devastating effect of a twenty-five pounder at every
road block, so that when they came " the b——s could be
blown to b—+—y." The wise platoon commander kept the
peace between them, and worried his company commander
for more weapons. He, in his turn, passed the buck upward
to his battalion commander, from whom it travelled by
devious ways to Whitehall.

But long before these necessary weapons were issued the
order went forth that the Home Guard must engage in
exercises with the regular troops training in the country,
in order that this amateur force should try its prentice hand
in mimic modern warfare. Prolonged drought during the
summer of 1940 had forced an exceptionally early harvest,
and so by the end of August the countryside was clear of
crops and the stage set for manœuvres.

One prevalent criticism of these operations in the countryside was that not enough attention was given to the small
exercise. This was understandable for two reasons.
Firstly, the High Command wanted to find out how the
Home Guard would co-operate with the regulars during a
big invasion ; and secondly, the majority of officers in the
Home Guard were retired brigadiers or at least colonels,
who were accustomed to thinking in terms of large forces.
So the average H.G. platoon often found itself part of a
sham fight on a twenty-mile front, and in the main hardly
knew whether it was going or coming during these operations.
But what the average rural platoon wanted to find out was
the best way for fifty Home Guards armed with rifles and
shot-guns to deal with a similar number of well-armed
German parachutists who had taken up their position in an
isolated set of farm buildings.

One thing that made these first exercises very keenly
contested on the part of the Home Guard was the then far
too prevalent feeling of disquiet concerning the efficiency
of the regular army. The old soldiers especially were very

outspoken in their criticisms. They expressed their disgust at the way in which the army had been turfed out of France, and informed everybody that in their day the British Army had stayed put in every country to which it had been sent until it chose to leave it. Consequently they were determined that in these manœuvres the Home Guard should give the regulars a run for their money.

Tales of those first exercises are many, and doubtless the results were fifty-fifty between regulars and Home Guard ; but, as a member of the latter, I must be forgiven for telling those that reflect credit on my own side. One thing, however, was noticeable in every exercise—that in both town and country the Home Guard showed up not as second-class soldiers but rather as first-class bandits. In other words, they did not play the game according to the rules.

For instance, one enthusiastic City Home Guard told me a great story of an exercise, in which the Home Guard had attacked the regulars. It was timed to begin at 9.30 A.M.—help ! at 0930 hours—and it was estimated that by 1200 hours things would be getting interesting. So the bigwigs decided to begin their investigation about that time. Alas ! By 1000 hours the Home Guard had their enemy's commanding officer tied to a chair in his head-quarters, having travelled a mile underground through the sewers of the City. Which, presumably, was hardly cricket, but very definitely good Home Guard tactics.

A Western County told me an even better one. There the regulars had agreed to attack a road block. Seeing that the defenders were but Home Guard, they did not think it necessary to send out scouts or to deploy off the road until they got within striking distance of their objective. But a mile and a half short of the road block the Home Guard set on them ; and, according to the umpires, scuppered them properly. Whereupon the regulars were very annoyed and said, " Look here, next time you agree to defend a something road block you defend it at the something road block or we shan't play."

One army trick that every civilian Home Guard soon learned from these exercises was the art of scrounging. The official issue of blank, of thunder-flashes, and all necessaries for them was very small and often non-existent ; so the good Home Guard officer and section leader supplemented it by devious means. Regulars were billeted in every house in the countryside, and the amount of useful stuff that their Home Guard war-time hosts coaxed out of them is nobody's business.

The shortage of rifles in every Home Guard platoon was another difficulty, for according to the regulations no rifles could be borrowed even for half a day. However, rifles were borrowed, even if the borrowers had to motor forty miles to get them, and swear, not only a vow of secrecy, but also to return them before nightfall. It was against the rules, but rules were never made for Home Guards.

The main point in every Home Guard leader's mind was that if his men were to lie doggo for half of Sunday, waiting to be attacked by regulars with lashings of blank and bombs, somehow or other his men were going to have something with which to make a noise, even if the authorities had ordained otherwise. So shot-gun cartridges were de-shotted, and those who possessed .45 revolvers were overjoyed to discover that 410 shot cartridges could be cut down into revolver blank quite easily.

" Where," asked the puzzled umpires of these exercises, " did the Home Guard get all this bally blank ? " If they could not guess nobody bothered to tell them.

Occasionally an exercise went sadly astray, in that it afforded no excitement for some of the men engaged in it. On one occasion the local Home Guard were given orders to man a position by 0830 hours one Sunday morning, and had been promised that they would be attacked strongly by a mobile column. They did this, and shortly afterwards their scouts reported that column a few miles to the west; so they sat tight and waited for them. They were armed to the teeth with quite three times the stuff that officialdom credited them, a half-dozen enthusiasts having spent the previous week in its collection.

There they waited, hour after hour while nothing happened. Literally nothing, for not even an umpire showed up to take any interest in them. The exercise was timed to end at 1230 hours, but at 1130 hours the H.G. runner, who had been sent to the Company H.Q., returned with the news that everybody had gone home, and that the battle was over. So the C.O. ordered a very disgruntled platoon to dismiss forthwith.

What really happened they never knew, but it was clear that there had been some muddle in the direction of this exercise, and that they had been shamefully overlooked by the higher command. So they groused—golly, how they groused. They said things about the British Army and their H.G. superiors that would have justified court-martial on the grounds that it was harmful to the public morale. Never mind; they said them, loud and long, and to such a tune that their C.O. took up the battle on their behalf on the Monday morning. It was useless for any Staff officer to apologize to him, saying that he was frightfully sorry and that he had no idea of what was happening. He was given to understand two things. Firstly, that it was his business to know what was happening; and secondly, that some sort of apology or explanation was due to the men, or in future exercises they would refuse to play.

Here be it said that the Staff played up, evidently realizing that Home Guard were a very different kettle of fish from regular troops. A few days later, when the platoon was waiting for a training film to begin, a Staff officer whom

D

everybody respected put the matter right in most charming fashion.

" There are," he informed them, " two different types of exercises. Some are exciting, and some are, frankly, dull." Here his audience snorted their agreement.

" Ah, I see you have some knowledge of the latter type. Well, you are not alone in that experience. Some months ago during a big army exercise a large body of troops by some mistake were forgotten completely. All day they had no fun, no excitement, and, worse than either, even their grub never turned up. To add to their miseries, in the evening it rained, and as they were marching along, wet through, tired, fed up, and hungry, one wag spoke his feelings aloud. ' Never before in the history of the British Army,' he said, ' have so many good men been mucked about so shamefully by so few.' "

Here he got the laugh he was angling for, and when it subsided he raised a louder one by remarking, " And, gentlemen, he didn't say ' mucked about.' "

" But the point is," he went on, " that even from the dullest exercise we can learn something. For instance, last Sunday we learned who was responsible for the mistake that gave you such a dull time after all your preparations. The fault was not yours, and I now assure you that it shall not happen again."

Which was, I think, as near an apology as even the most disgruntled man could expect a regular Staff officer to make to N.C.O.'s and men of the Home Guard. Also it did suggest that perhaps the High Command valued the Home Guard more highly than they did themselves. Anyway, during those early exercises there is no doubt that to each platoon came its little triumphs and defeats, annoyances and lessons.

Of course, Sedgebury Wallop shared in these. In late August, orders came through that on the following Sunday morning the village was to be attacked by a local striking-force of regulars, and a few days before Sir Robert Enfield was in conference with his section leaders.

" Must put up a good show, Pocock," he was saying. " These strikin'-force fellas are as keen as mustard, so we shall have our work cut out. Now here is the plan. Although they are what is known as a mechanized unit, for this exercise they will operate as infantry. They will drive out to a map reference, debus—horrible word—and attack us on foot from the west. Now, where is the map ? Ah, you have one, Butler. Good."

The Squire fumbled among his papers for a few moments.

" Ah, here we are. The unit will rendezvous at 516534. Now where exactly is that, Butler ? "

Tom spread the map out on the desk and pointed to the correct spot.

" Quite so, quite so. Got that, Pocock ? "

" Yes, sir. What we call Six Ways. Favourite beat for woodcock. From there it'll take 'em a good half-hour on foot to get in touch with Wallop."

" Yes, that is part of the show, Pocock. Their C.O., Major Loder, told me that a walk would do his men a lot of good. Said they'd almost forgotten the way to use their feet. Now we shall defend the village at our road block at the cross-roads. I want you two to work out a plan, and we'll settle it finally on Saturday evening."

Tom Butler then raised the question of blank.

" Not a hope, Butler," came the reply. " I've done my best, but I couldn't get one round. So we shall have to rely on the umpires knowing their job."

" And you might as well rely on rain going upward," snarled Tom to his friend as they were driving away. " Without blank any exercise is a farce, and without blank the men will consider it a waste of time. Get 'em once like that, and the second time they won't play."

" Never mind. It'll be the same for both sides," said Walter.

" Like hell it will. I've met Major Loder. He's taken a farmhouse t'other side of Yarborough, and keeps some poultry. Coaxed me to let him have some food for 'em, too. I tell you that fellow knows his way about, and whatever he don't do on Sunday his men'll have blank. And not only blank, but thunder-flashes, smoke-bombs, gas-bombs, and all sorts. You'll see. And our chaps'll have to stay put like fools with nothing to tell anybody that they're in the battle at all."

" Then they can't be blamed for losing it," comforted Walter. " But, Tom, what does worry me far more than having no blank is that Squire intends to stay at platoon headquarters all the time. I mean, how can he run a little fight like this from an office ? "

" He can't. But, bless you, damn near all the officers in the Home Guard are ex-high-up regulars. I tell you, Walter, the last war was a subaltern's war, and this Home Guard stunt'll be a sergeant's job. Anyway, that's what it'll be on Sunday—two sergeants, fifty Home Guard, no blank, but a hell of a lot of hope. But don't worry, Walter, it'll all be over by twelve o'clock, and whether we work hard or not the result will be the same."

" How d'you mean, Tom ? "

" The umpires will report that both sides deserved great credit. Bless you, they always do. So cheer up."

Tom Butler hopped out of the car at the mill gate, and a mystified Home Guard sergeant then drove slowly homeward. It was all very well for Tom to tell him not to worry, but, dash it, somebody ought to worry. This was supposed to be a rehearsal of the real thing, a necessary rehearsal, too. It wouldn't be all right unless somebody worried. Well, in spite of Tom's advice, he would worry. There might be no blank, but surely this attack would teach him whether his men were placed to the best advantage. How should they be placed ? To find the correct answer to that question should be this week's worry.

By Friday night he had worried out what he considered to be a satisfactory answer, and the appearance of Major Loder in a light army lorry in Wallop and its outskirts on the Saturday morning brought a grim smile to Walter's face.

" H'm," he muttered. " What they call a reconnaissance party, I reckon. Well, we'll let 'em get on with it. Fred "— this to Carter Goodridge, who was leading a horse and cart out of the main gates of the Manor Farm—" I've changed my mind. We won't do that job now. You finish out the morning collecting those hedge-trimmings, and we'll put in some overtime this afternoon."

The result of their overtime some hours later was that on Sunday morning Sedgebury Wallop wore the same comfortable look as it had done in pre-war days. Gone were the dug-outs and pill-boxes so proudly and hastily constructed some months before, and not one sandbag was left to show that the village was at war.

" An' I 'low as we carted all o' ten ton o' sand time we was done," Fred Goodridge informed the company at the Wheatsheaf on Saturday evening. " Well, I don't know wot caper Maister Pocock be playin' at, but the village do look a sight tidier because ov it."

" Don't matter wot the guv'ner do do, Fred," mourned Shep Yates. " Wi'out any blank to-morrow'll be a wash-out."

Even Tom Butler was puzzled at his friend's unusual activity, and said as much.

" You sort of allergic to sandbags, Walter ? " he inquired that same evening during a secret session with his co-sergeant.

" No," grunted Walter. " But if the enemy only is to

have blank I don't see the sense of marking out our positions for him to shoot at. We'll place our men so that the village street looks just the same as it did in peace-time, and watch how the blank fizzes on that."

But though Tom Butler agreed to his friend's plan, Walter had a hard job on Saturday evening to convince his platoon commander that the removal of all obvious war-like preparations from the village was sound strategy. However, as there was no time to fill and replace the sandbags, the Squire drove back to his H.Q. full of misgivings concerning the coming battle.

At 0900 hours the cars and lorries of the striking-force rumbled around the village and up the hill towards Ludcombe Wood, and half an hour later the Home Guard paraded on the green. The section leaders posted their men, impressing on every one the paramount necessity to keep well hidden.

"This ain't war," remarked Tom to his braves. "In fact it ain't even manœuvres nor an exercise. It's just plain foolery wi' one side makin' a noise, and t'other not allowed even a pop-gun. So, my sons, you will keep your flaming heads down and lie doggo. Let the bloomin' strikin'-force take the village. This battle ain't goin' to be won by shootin' but by talkin' afterwards, and the Home Guard can talk any regular out of anything."

According to plan the striking-force came down like a wolf on the fold. Early in the attack it captured a very frightened cyclist scout in Lightnin' Bridle, and on the outskirts of the village it easily scuppered a too obvious forward observation post. Then the attackers deployed and swarmed into the west side of the village along every path and alleyway, shooting and bombing as they came.

"Noisy little fellers, ain't they, Walt?" muttered Tom Butler, as he and his friend crouched behind a low wall at the cross-roads by the Wheatsheaf Inn. " Reg'lar Guy Fawkes for 'em this morning."

Walter merely grunted, and watched the attack develop. He saw enemy soldiers creeping out of this garden gate, and that footpath. He listened to their shots. He noticed the young officer leading the attack stop every few yards and hurl a thunder-flash that exploded fifteen seconds later with a most realistic thump.

" Some day," he thought, " I may see this happen in reality. Those chaps won't be the local striking-force, they'll be real enemy—Germans. Those bombs won't be just fireworks but dangerous. Those shots will be ball not blank. And what happens to the village and to the Home Guard will be largely my fault. It's my responsibility. And I don't know enough about this game to shoulder it. Well, how wrong are the men's placings this morning ? "

So interested was he in the picture of the future that his imagination was busy painting from the actual scene in front of him that he forgot to stay under cover, and forgot also that he was supposed to be a soldier of sorts. Instead, he stepped out on to the pavement, and leaned in comfort against the wall that had hidden him, surveying the enemy attack as it surged down the village street towards the cross-roads.

" Walt, you B.F.," admonished Tom from behind the wall. " You'll get ticked off proper for exposing yourself like that. Anyway, what's the idea ? "

" Nothin', only that if you haven't got any blank to fight with you may as well be careful to watch how the experts use it," came the reply.

Along came the attack, emitting increasing noise at every step. Presently it reached the cross-roads, and a lighted thunder-flash was hurled to within a couple of yards of an apparently lazy Home Guard. Walter watched it carefully until it exploded, and then turned to be greeted by a scornful subaltern.

" And what in hell d'you think you're doing, sergeant ? " asked the officer. " Waiting for the pub to open ? "

" No, sir," said Walter, coming to attention and giving his questioner an awkward salute. " Just making careful notes to tell the umpire how you led your men within a few yards of my riflemen. You see, we haven't any blank."

" Your riflemen ? Apart from the four we captured outside the village we haven't seen one. This block isn't defended at all."

" I'm sorry, sir, but some fifty men in cover would have been shooting at your men for the last twenty minutes."

" The devil they would ! Here, come and show me."

Walter showed him riflemen everywhere—in lofts, cowhouses, and woodsheds, with nothing to mark their presence, not even a loop-hole, for the rifle-muzzles peeped through gaps in weather-boards and broken brickwork.

" H'm," muttered the officer to himself. " Not even one bloody sandbag nor one bit of camouflage to mark the spot. We'd have been scuppered all right. Why, damn it, my own section passed within three yards of those two riflemen." And then aloud, " All right, sergeant. I reckon you win, and I shall report to the umpires to that effect. Ah, here they come—as ever, too late to see anything. But don't you worry, sergeant. Wallop's won."

CHAPTER 5

Alarums and Excursions

WITHOUT warning, during the first week-end of September 1940, came the threat of invasion. On that Saturday afternoon, evening, and all night the Luftwaffe carried out its first real blitz on London. The enemy bombed that city almost continuously from 3 P.M. until about 3 A.M. Here I do not speak from hearsay, as I was sleeping at my club in order to keep a broadcasting engagement timed for 8.30 on Sunday morning.

Not having enough military knowledge to know what was happening, I played bridge until the first " All Clear " at about seven o'clock. Then, finding that a friend and fellow-member, Commander Kenneth Edwards, R.N., agreed with me that September spelt oysters, we set out to find some. As we crossed Piccadilly the siren sounded again, but we both agreed that as this might well be our last chance of oysters, the thing to do was to walk on to Bentley's. There my companion found an old shipmate behind the bar who said that in spite of the Luftwaffe he would open oysters as long as we would pay for them, so we did our best, and a good best it was. We then went our several ways.

Later on when I was back at the club the blitz began in earnest, and continued throughout that long summer night. We soon decided that a card-room three stories up was not the best place under the circumstances, and retired to the basement to continue the game. After a while bridge did not seem to be so interesting as usual, so every now and again some of us went outside to watch. We heard the crack of ack-ack guns and the heavy crump of enemy bombs. The attack seemed to be mainly along the river, and soon we were to see a glow in the sky as though the whole of the east of London was on fire. Somewhere about two o'clock there was a lull, and one or two of us crept along the street with the idea of getting some bacon and eggs at a Corner House. But before we had gone fifty yards a bomb dropped somewhere the other side of the river, but close enough to make us hesitate ; whereupon a constable advised us that bacon and eggs might be dearly bought. So we retired to the club basement, and gave both the Luftwaffe and the bridge-table best for a while.

All that may sound silly, callous, and impossible, but I am telling it just as it happened. Also the time factor must be considered. At that date no one had experienced night bombing and therefore we did not realize what was happening. At that date one could buy bacon and eggs at will. At that date one could motor up to London occasionally, and perhaps enjoy some oysters.

Anyway, that was my end of it, and I drove away from Langham Place at nine o'clock next morning in complete ignorance of what had happened in the countryside. Once out of London I was stopped by regular soldiers or Home Guards at every bend in the road until I arrived at Salisbury. This could not be merely a local exercise, so just west of Staines I inquired the reason from a regular sergeant. " Don't rightly know," he said. " But there's one hell of a flap on, and we've been stood to all night. You'd best go careful."

To this day I do not know what exactly did happen, but rumour informed me that at some point during that first blitz on London some one rang some church bells somewhere in the south of England, with the result that the alarm spread from London to Bristol and beyond. Whether there was a genuine threat of invasion or not nobody seemed to know for certain, and to date the future has brought me no definite evidence either way. But I do know that the Home Guard stood to at their posts through that long warm fateful night, and that round every bend and at every cross-roads I found them with loaded rifles and itching trigger fingers. And I, an enthusiastic Home Guard, had missed this first real job of work, simply because I had been broadcasting. Somehow that hurt.

However, there is no doubt at all that the Home Guard all over Britain were disappointed that the alarm proved to be a false one; although, dear knows, that at that date they were ill-equipped to deal with enemy invasion. For instance, the Sedgebury Wallop platoon was on the job that night, and this unit marched seventeen bewildered civilians to the local police-station because they had forgotten their identity cards. Their captors wanted no argument but immediate obedience, and saw to it that this was forthcoming. But at 0700 hours the farmer in Walter Pocock woke up, and suggested to his shepherd that he might abandon soldiering for shepherding for half an hour.

" You'll be wantin' to see your sheep, but take your rifle and ammo," he advised. " The fold's only ten minutes' walk away, and I'll send for you the moment anything happens."

" I 'low me sheep'll be all right eet awhile," retorted Shep. " The day's fold were pitched eesterday, an' although young Arthur be but fifteen, I've a-trained 'im proper. Any road, I bain't gwaine till the ' All Clear ' be sounded."

Which was the general opinion throughout the platoon, and obviously an indication of the behaviour of Home Guards throughout Britain on that memorable Sunday morning. In fact, about eleven o'clock, when the word came through that the real or imaginary threat of invasion had passed, the grumbling was rife.

" Bain't 'em reely comin', sir ? " asked Tom Spicer wistfully, when he heard the sad news.

" 'Fraid not, Spicer," replied Walter, who by this time

had hardly decided whether to be relieved or disappointed at the outcome of the alarm.

" Jist wot I thought," growled Fred Bunce, the blacksmith. " There ain't no dependence to be put in they Germans."

" You be right there, Fred," chimed in Shep Yates. " I feared as much, an' it 'ave 'appened. The zods 'ave let us down proper. Yer we bin, 'angin' about fur nigh on twelve hours, an' all fur nothin'."

But it wasn't all for nothing. That first invasion scare told everybody that any day these part-time soldiers might suddenly find themselves on active service, and it did something else even more valuable. It hurried up the issue of new weapons. By October the loss of arms and equipment of the regular army at Dunkirk had been largely made good, and the news came through that automatic weapons, mostly American-type Lewis guns, were to be issued. So during that month at every military camp in England on Sunday mornings the Home Guard gathered to collect the new weapons and instruction in how to use them.

Usually two N.C.O.'s from each platoon were sent on this job, which meant that perhaps fifty Home Guards spent a Sunday morning hanging on to every word of wisdom from the instructor. But when, having taken a gun to pieces and scattered its innards on the cement floor of a hut, this wizard called for volunteers to put it together again there was always a rush of would-be experts to try their hands. Having learned all they could in the time allotted, they packed the guns in their cars and went home, not to take their wives to church, I'm afraid, but to play with their new toys on the sitting-room floor until late at night, or rather until their wives let them know beyond all question who was really the O.C. of the home.

Most of the rural Home Guard, from officer to private, were familiar with machinery; and where the C.O. of a platoon had unfortunately been deprived of such knowledge by chauffeurs, gamekeepers, and other servants, he very wisely admitted his deficiencies, and left it to those under him who had learned by experience through both hands and head.

When these enthusiasts found themselves stuck they shamelessly pressed into service the regular troops near by. The bombardier of a searchlight post suddenly found himself instructing in machine-gun lore in the farmhouse kitchen. Any soldier who admitted to knowledge of a Lewis gun might obey orders by day, but gave orders in the village hall in the evening; while the Lewis gunner who had the misfortune to be billeted with a would-be H.G. machine-gunner suddenly discovered that this war meant for him a twenty-four-hour day. He might help to fight the enemy by day, but he was certain to have to fight his H.G. host at night.

There were also the individualists, who vowed that no blooming Yankee gun could defeat them. For instance, I know one farmer in Hampshire, then a section leader, to whom was delivered a machine-gun in a box, together with a supply of ammunition, with a note to the effect that in due course an instructor would be forthcoming. " In due course ? " No Home Guard could wait for that. So he prised open the box, to find the gun dismantled, but to his great joy a book of instructions.

That evening he worried that book and those parts until he had the gun together, and seemingly in working order. Next morning he blew off some twenty rounds into a hayrick just to prove that the gun had been assembled correctly. Then within a week by evening instruction he had trained his section to similar efficiency, a job that, to use his own words, " would have taken the army three months." Subsequently the army instructor did show him that he had a lot to learn and he learned it, but the point is that a few hours after the arrival of that gun one novice could have made it work if the need had arisen. Not good soldiering, may be, but definitely good Home Guard.

This issue of automatic weapons in the autumn of 1940 increased the fire-power of the Home Guard tremendously. In my own district no platoon received less than two L.M.G.'s of sorts, and some had three or four. Put the average per platoon at two and a half, then multiply this by the number of villages in Britain, in the south of England one village every three miles, and some idea of the fire-power of this part-time force can be obtained.

Other arms and equipment now began to come along in steadily increasing supply. The .303 rifles were replaced by American Springfields .300. This was a sound move from a military angle, as it meant that the Home Guard's rifles and machine-guns now took the same ammunition ; but the men regretted losing a rifle that they had cherished, especially those who had somehow managed to obtain a short Lee Enfield. Mills grenades, too, were issued, and a small supply of dummies for training purposes.

The most popular intake was a steady trickle of overcoats and serge battle-dress to replace the ill-fitting and cold denims. Most of these serge uniforms were made for slim men, and so middle-aged rotundity had to wait for months, while those whom they described as " herring-gutted " paraded proudly, looking like real soldiers. However, there is always a *modus vivendi* in rural districts, so the more corpulent N.C.O.'s, such as myself, broke the regulations in order to clothe ourselves as befitted our rank and responsibilities. As soon as the supply warranted it we bagged a suit and a half, and sometimes two apiece, took these to the local tailor, and informed him that the war might be lost if out of two suits he could not make a suit to cover us fittingly.

The Home Guard then settled down to serious weapon training during its first winter. At the end of October the all night observation duty ceased, simply because at the critical hours of dusk and dawn men had to be at their civil work. So selected N.C.O.'s and men were sent on week-end courses to near-by military camps, and returned home to spread the light among their companions. In village halls, schoolrooms, and even in barns, men could be found learning the mysteries of machine-guns and grenades, often by the indifferent light of hurricane lanterns. Beer and cigarettes were wagered on speed in stripping and assembly, and the rural aptitude for machinery and gambling made these competitions almost too popular.

It was the ex-soldiers who pointed this out, and demanded more training in the tactical use of the new weapons. When no outside lecturer was available they became amateur schoolmasters for one hot smoky hour, and even drew curious diagrams on the blackboard to illustrate their lessons. Their methods were unorthodox, and their language often unprintable, but they got their points home. Here is a revised version of one ex-soldier N.C.O.'s delivery.

" I know you can strip the gun and assemble it in so many seconds, which is a good thing to be able to do. But that gun's made for use, to fight with. How the hell do we know that Jerry'll come in daylight? P'raps one night I'll be sittin' behind that gun bellowin' for another full magazine, and God help the bloke that can't produce it. So, my sons, we'll put out all lights and practise fillin' mags in the dark."

Having got his machine-gun team trained more or less to his liking, he then practised them going into action with the gun in daylight until they got so bored with this job that they kicked.

" You know how to do that, do you? " he countered. " Of course you do, in daylight, with me barkin' at you. But you must carry on doing it until you can do it dead, drunk, sober, or damned. I know the old army training is supposed to be out of date, and that every private soldier is now supposed to be a command on his own. But there is something in the old method, so you must train so that you can do this job automatically when you hear a familiar command, even though all hell's breakin' round you. That ain't easy, and there ain't time to think it out. So you'll carry on with this boring job until I've got you like the old naval pensioner."

" What happened to him, Serge ? " inquired a hopeful recruit.

" Oh, he was an old gunner, and he was sitting in his cottage in front of the fire reading the newspaper. Presently he dozed off, the paper slipped into the fire, and caught alight. His old wife saw this, and cried out, ' John ! Fire ! ' The old chap jumped up on the instant, opened the oven door, shoved in the cat, slammed the door, turned the handle, and shouted, ' Ready ! ' Then, when that was done, he really woke up."

As a civilian Home Guard I am inclined to agree with that sergeant that there still is much to be said in favour of the old type of army training, whereby the trainee becomes able to do certain essential things without thinking and under any circumstances.

It is difficult to give a true estimate of the work that many ex-soldier Home Guard section leaders did and still do, but here is an average week during that first winter. Sunday—away all day at a course of instruction at a near-by camp. Monday—drive to Platoon H.Q., collect an issue of equipment, and spend the evening dishing it out to various men. Tuesday evening—attend training film or lecture. Wednesday evening—either bow to major force and take wife to pictures, or spend several hours working out a scheme for next Sunday. Thursday evening—miniature rifle-range. Friday evening—another dose of equipment to deal with. Saturday evening—perfect arrangements for the morrow's exercise. That sort of thing went on week after week, and meant perhaps thirty hours a week at Home Guard duties in addition to civilian work that each week became more arduous.

Here, I think, I must pay some tribute to the police force. In every rural district they were the Home Guard's father, mother, and teacher. In addition to the enormous amount of extra work that the war had thrust on them, the local police inspectors found time to train the Home Guard in the right way to deal with incendiary bombs, and in the correct use of the respirator, and helped in every possible way. True, in return the Home Guard did arrange to provide squads of trained men under control of N.C.O.'s at the call of the police should any night attack from the air be made on the locality. In addition, the First Aid Detachments, the A.R.P., and all the local Civil Defence services helped and worked with the Home Guard, so that it was never in a watertight compartment. Later on the military authorities were able to arrange full training in all these things for the Home Guard, but during that first winter it was the local police and Civil Defence services that gave the Home Guard its first lessons.

In some districts one or two Home Guard units were lucky enough to experience a taste of actual warfare. For instance, one platoon in the South Eastern Command was credited with having brought down an enemy plane by rifle-fire; b it up to date only one operation that could be called at all exciting has come my way. One dark winter night about ten o'clock, just as I was going upstairs to bed, I received a message by telephone to the effect that a German airman who had baled out some days before had been seen some seven miles away. So I grabbed greatcoat, gum-boots, and arms, and in a few minutes had the cross-roads blocked by half a dozen men, and two car-loads scouting up different roads.

In perhaps a dozen neighbouring villages other Home Guards did the same, and by eleven o'clock the quarry was

E

captured, unfortunately not by my squad. However, a car from a neighbouring platoon reported that the man was now in the local police-station, so we set off to try to have a look at him. Incidentally, to see six stalwart rural Home Guards emerge from a Ford ten, all complete with rifles and fixed bayonets, is an awe-inspiring sight.

Presently I joined a mixed company in the local police-station that was filled almost to bursting-point. There were ten or a dozen Home Guards, three police constables, and one police sergeant busy at the telephone. In the middle of this gathering on a wooden kitchen chair sat the prisoner, steadily eating bread and butter, while most of us wished that the sergeant would hurry up with his telephoning so that we could inquire details of his capture.

The prisoner was a young man about twenty-three, not at all the bogey of so many people's imaginations, but a very ordinary, decent-looking lad. There was a curious dignity about him, too, and I wondered whether I should have been able to acquit myself so well in a comparable situation in Germany. Frankly, I doubted this very much.

Still, I could not help thinking that the German equivalent of the plight in which this lad now found himself would probably be much more terrifying. Anyway, neither the policemen nor the Home Guards in that little room could have appeared very awe-inspiring. In fact, if truth be told, the whole business was obviously as new and as puzzling to the captors as to the captive. However, as these thoughts were passing through my mind the door of the police-station suddenly opened, and in came an intelligence officer. He immediately took charge of the proceedings, which meant that such humble folk as Home Guard spectators quietly faded away outside into the night.

As I was driving home I realized that I, a civilian, had just experienced my first taste of war, and that I disliked it intensely. I was dead keen to hunt that fellow, felt the same exhilaration as I did when hounds were running, and would have shot him on the instant if need be. But, somehow, when he was caught I had no further quarrel with him.

True, I had no sympathy with either him or his cause, yet in spite of his horrible trade, the night bombing of civilians of all ages and sexes, I could not help admiring him. For in my eyes any man who flew a plane at night from Germany to here or the other way round was a brave man. So I decided then and there I would prefer to meet the enemy fighting than as a prisoner. While he fights I can try to kill him without a qualm, but when he is taken prisoner he changes from a fighting enemy to a forlorn boy, and—well, I cannot deal with him. In fact, he defeats me entirely. Undoubtedly the reason for this rather curious attitude is because in modern war the actual killing of an enemy is largely impersonal, accomplished by soldiers either at long range or in the throes of great excitement, while taking an enemy prisoner must generally be a rather personal matter between two human beings.

Apart from these personal wonderings that incident seemed to me to prove the efficiency of the Home Guard. Although some of the men I called were in bed, they were dressed more or less in uniform and on the job in a few minutes. This happened in perhaps a dozen adjoining villages, which meant that the airman had little chance of escape, for the Home Guard were better fitted for this particular type of hunting by night than ten times their number of regulars. In every village they knew who might have reason to be walking late at night, and in most cases could recognize their neighbours by the sound of their steps. But a strange step, a strange voice, or a strange shape were immediately suspect, even in the dark.

During that first winter the Home Guard often got a chance to watch the regulars at their exercises, usually by official arrangement, but sometimes by grace and favour.

For instance, one evening Major Trench, who had been billeted for some months at the Manor Farm, Sedgebury Wallop, asked Walter Pocock whether he would like to watch some early morning manœuvres on Salisbury Plain.

" All rightfully hush-hush in a way," he said, " but I think I can wangle you a pass, Walter."

" What precisely's on ? " Walter inquired.

" Birds. In the exercise that's in progress one side's dropping some parachute troops behind the others' lines. Gives us all a chance to see how that sort of thing works, how quick our aircraft can be on the scene after the alarm, and all sorts. The G.O.C., princes, foreign attachés, politicians, generals galore—in fact, all the big stuff will be there to watch."

" H'm ! Many Home Guards to be present ? "

" None so far as I know."

" But I thought our main job was to deal with parachute troops ? Surely a selection of Home Guard officers ought to be invited to watch this display ? "

" Walter, you've too logical a mind. They should, but the fact remains that they haven't been asked."

" I see. Then I shall be the only Home Guard present ? Bit of an ordeal for one Home Guard sergeant. How'd you like to join the rank and flower of the British Army, Navy, Air Force, and aristocracy, to say nothing of crowned heads and politicians, in my sergeant's denim uniform ? Make it a pass for two, Frank, so that I can take a pal to keep me company."

" All right, I will. But you must both be in uniform. And don't tell your pal where or why he's going until you've got him in the car on Tuesday morning. Then he cannot give it away. We've enough worry with this job without a crowd of unauthorized sightseers."

" How d'you mean ? "

" Well, we've had to muzzle the local Home Guard, and

the vicars, and the vergers, and the bell-ringers. Else when our birds begin to fall they'll assume the invasion's begun and ring everything in sight."

At this Walter chuckled aloud.

" You may laugh, Walter, but it's no laughing matter. True, we have managed to muzzle the locals, but we cannot legislate for the motorist coming up from the west at dawn on Tuesday morning. When he sees our birds he'll drive furiously to the nearest police-station and raise Cain and Abel."

At one hour before dawn Walter drove steadily out of Sedgebury Wallop with Tom Butler sitting by his side.

" And now what's the programme, Walter ? " demanded Tom. " Battle, murder, or sudden death ? "

" May be all three," replied Walter, and then proceeded to let his friend into the secret of the day's doings.

" Ster-ewth ! " chortled Tom. " Ain't we the favoured few ? Next week I seem to hear a lecture by Sergeant Pocock on the correct way of shooting a Jerry parachute trooper in the posterior as he floats to earth. Golly, Walter, I know hundreds of Home Guards who'd give their eyes for this chance."

When they arrived at the rendezvous a military policeman examined their passes, and then directed them where to park their car.

" You will have about a mile to walk, sir. Up that drove over the downs. Just follow the other gentlemen."

Walter thanked him, and drove to the parking place, his friend chuckling the while.

" And what's amusing you, Tom ? "

" Nothing. Only that it's the first time I've ever heard a red-cap say ' Sir ' to a sergeant. The Home Guard's responsible for many queer things, Walter."

As Walter was locking his car preparatory to walking up the hill he spied his shooting-stick on the back seat.

"You know, Tom, I've half a mind to take my shooting-stick. I'm like the Irishman—I'd sooner walk ten miles than stand five, and this'll most likely be a standing job."

"Walter, you can't," said Tom, all the old soldier in him horrified at the very thought of such a thing.

"Can't I?" said Walter, reaching for the stick.

"Listen, Walt. You've never been a soldier, you never will be a soldier, and, God help me, you'll never even look like a soldier. But for this morning at least, do please try to behave like one as much as possible. And soldiers don't carry shooting-sticks, see? Moreover, from what you tell me the G.O.C. and one hell of a hoo-ha of officers will be up yonder, so a shooting-stick's impossible."

"Not a bit of it. Very useful tool this'll be this morning," and Walter held firmly to the offending stick.

"Then for my sake, Walt. For my sake don't take the bally thing. I'll not be seen with you. Walter, this is soldiering; you just can't."

"Can't I? You watch me try. Shouldn't wonder but what twenty folk'll want to buy this off me before the job's over. Besides, I ain't a soldier; I'm a Home Guard. Which is different, believe me. When my grandchildren ask me what I did in the Great War I shall tell 'em I took a shooting-stick to this show. Come on, Tom, I'll take the blame."

In great disgust Tom accompanied him up the hill, and after a quarter of an hour's plodding they reached a gathering of perhaps two hundred people in the middle of a vast expanse of open downland. As befitted their humble rank they drew off some fifty yards or so away from this company, whereupon Walter opened his shooting-stick, and planted his bottom firmly upon it, while Tom groaned aloud.

A few moments later Major Trench ambled across to greet them.

"Glad you found the spot all right, Walter. Only

another ten minutes before our birds'll arrive. I say, what's your friend Butler looking so glum about ? "

" My shooting-stick, Frank," chuckled Walter. " He doesn't consider it part of a good Home Guard's equipment. Hope I haven't let you and the whole party down by bringing it ? "

" On the contrary," laughed Trench. " When the G.O.C. spotted it a few moments ago, he said, ' Good God ! There's a feller sittin' on a shootin'-stick.' Then he took a good look at you, Walter, and said, ' H'm, it's a Home Guard. Only feller with any sense in the whole party.' Walter, you've made history. But I must get back now ; the birds'll be along any minute now."

The birds came. Enormous aircraft surged out of the misty wrack of the dawn and flew slowly overhead about four hundred feet up. From each a dozen or more para-chute troops dropped. All came to earth safely, ran to their arms container, and in a few moments were doubling away down the hill to attack the village.

Aircraft called up by wireless now swooped and dived at the company, but before they arrived the parachutists were safely away in cover.

" We'll need to get at those chaps quickly if they do come, Walter," remarked Tom.

" Yes. I timed 'em. They took less than thirty seconds to come to earth, and in a hundred and thirteen seconds one lot had fallen, clicked off their parachute harness, armed themselves from the container, and were away on business. Don't give anyone much time for anything. Tom, we need better discipline and fire control. We need a mobile squad to move out on the jump in cars or on bikes. What don't we need ? Come on, this has given us lots to get on with at home."

But as they walked down the hill towards the village Walter saw something that comforted him tremendously.

This was a farm workman driving a tractor steadily up and down, ploughing up a pasture field.

" It won't be so bad as I thought," he said aloud.

" How d'you mean, Walter ? "

" That chap with the tractor. He came out here at seven. Those chaps fell out of the sky as soon as it was light enough, say at eight o'clock. If they had been Germans, before they landed even that chap would have been away down the village with the alarm. With that rubber-tyred tractor he can travel a good twelve miles an hour cross-country."

But, when they reached the village and learned that the parachute troops had made off with a general's car that had been left unattended and not immobilized, two Home Guard sergeants realized once again how swift and surprising was this new method of attack by air-borne troops.

" Come on, Walt," said Tom Butler, " let's get back to work. We Home Guards ain't got much money, but we have got a shooting-stick."

CHAPTER 6

Visiting Rounds

BY 1941 the Home Guard had become an accepted part of the national life, a volunteer force still needing further training, but one that in the eyes of the military authorities was a valuable part of Britain's home defence. It had also established a definite form of freemasonry amongst its members, and in every lodge, or rather every platoon, visitors from other platoons were welcome. In short, Home Guard membership was a passport to almost any gathering of men, and, as one enthusiast put it, " When you've got retired colonels as privates, and lay preachers putting up stripes, friendship booms."

So, whenever business or scanty leisure permitted, Home Guards of every type visited other platoons and companies in order to collect valuable tips and to compare notes. But before I describe such visits as I was privileged to enjoy I must refer to one type of visit that worried me considerably. In the spring of 1941 I became a platoon officer, either as a reward of merit, because the work had increased to demand a second officer in the platoon, or in order to keep a bolshevistic sergeant quiet. I try to think that the first reason was responsible ; I know the second had some force ; and I now realize that the third came to pass. Responsibility is a wonderful brake.

Anyway, ignorant amateur though I was, it was up to me to try to do the job. As soon as the H.G. Observation Posts were again manned all night all over Britain one of my duties was to visit the local one at all hours between dusk and dawn. What happened to similar unfortunates in other platoons I know not, but this is how I was educated.

I would leave my car perhaps a quarter-mile from the post, and then walk, giving the customary recognition signal with my torch at due distance. When the squad was in charge of an ex-soldier or an amateur who had spared no pains to learn his new job I would be challenged and dealt with correctly. But occasionally after my signal I would hear something like this.

" Bill, there's some silly so-and-so movin' about out there." And then I would hear the rifle bolts go up with that ominous *clop*. Remembering that every man on the post carried forty rounds of ball ammunition, and that the majority were indeed amateur soldiers, I used to gulp, take a deep breath, and paddle onward. The danger could not have been very real, for I am still alive to tell the tale after perhaps a dozen such hazards, but I soon decided that some further training in the duties of a sentry was advisable for everybody's safety.

At first when I suggested this to my C.O. he seemed to think that I, the civilian, was demanding too much militarism, something to which the average civilian Home Guard was rather prone in those days. But when, after going through the strength lists, I was able to point out that two-thirds of his command possessed no previous military experience whatsoever, he gave orders that the old soldiers should each take a squad of amateurs on the following Sunday morning and teach them the whole duty of a sentry.

He also got out a set of orders for the operation of the O.P., and posted these in the hut. This was a good move, for until then the N.C.O. in charge had had no real authority. Now he could refer to a list of instructions signed by his C.O., and insist on their being carried out.

Those night visits during the summer of 1941 were a strange experience for a farmer. Sometimes I would stay up late, and visit the post at 0100 hours. Sometimes I would go to bed early and make the trip an hour before dawn, say at 0430 hours. Sometimes I depended on an alarm clock to waken me in the middle of the night. And —for truth must be told—sometimes the bed pulled so strongly that I used to reach out one arm and ring up, for the post was on the telephone.

In the beginning I had thought that the men would be likely to resent my night visiting at all hours, on the grounds that it was done in order to catch them out, and implied that their officers' mistrusted them. But I was mistaken. Before long it was evident that such visits were welcome, and for two reasons. One was that they relieved the boredom of the night ; and the other that they showed that a continuous interest was being taken in their job by those responsible for its being done. What was the correct manner of making these visiting rounds, or how others did them, I shall never know. It was obvious that the visit of a martinet schoolmaster trying to catch out small boys would be worse than useless. To me the Haroun-Al-Raschid attitude savoured of snobbery. So, rightly or wrongly, once the first challenge had been properly dealt with I yarned with my equals for sometimes an hour concerning the better running of the platoon or the happenings in the night sky.

From the top of the downs we watched raids on a coastal town, perhaps a bare twenty miles distant, reported occasional strange lights, and listened to the roar of our night-fighters overhead. But nothing really exciting came our way that summer ; and so, when with the coming of winter the night Observation Posts were once again abandoned I was able to visit the Home Guard outside my native Wiltshire. My friend, Major Charles Hambourg, had kindly offered to let me see his company at work in London, and one December day I was able to accept this invitation.

During the afternoon I was given a rough outline of the defence of London by the Home Guard, and also an insight into its administration. Like the countryside, this vast city had been divided into sub-areas, and these into zones, each zone being manned by a brigade of three battalions. Each battalion was divided into four companies, each of three platoons; and in addition there were factory units of Home Guard, whose first job was to defend their own factories. Should enemy action put a factory out of action its Home Guard were to report immediately to its Battalion H.Q. Broadly speaking, it seemed that the static defence of London was in the hands of the Home Guard, leaving regular troops as mobile defenders.

As in the country, the early arrangements in London had obeyed no specific rule, but were carried out by enthusiastic soldiers. Thus my friend had somehow been authorized to form a company of three hundred and fifty men, had interviewed each applicant at a police-station, and selected his N.C.O.'s. Subsequently, when arrangements had been made for training, at his own expense he had called up the men by circular. That afternoon I saw a Battalion H.Q. organized to the last detail, but I realized that the early start and after-success of the Home Guard had mainly depended on the unselfish work of hundreds of ex-soldiers.

They arranged for tailors to measure their men, indented for uniforms, and worried the life out of those responsible for not sending them. But, uniforms or no uniforms, they got on with the training, sending batches of men to Bisley on Sundays for firing practice even when rifles were few and far between, and practice ammunition a minus quantity.

But I wanted to see the men at their training, and said as much; so my friend, his second-in-command, and myself dined together that evening, and then set out in his car to the training depot of his old company. Just where that is, or was, I do not rightly know. The car wound through the winter dark of war-time London, northward to Piccadilly Circus, and thence, for I am a country Home Guard, in a northerly direction with perhaps a touch of west in it, seemingly through miles and miles of uncharted streets. In two minutes I was lost completely, and all I know about the route is that we passed two prisons.

Eventually the car was parked in the playground of a school, its top floor now a Home Guard Company H.Q., for its scholars had long since been evacuated to the countryside. So we went up several flights of stairs, and were challenged in proper form at the door leading to the scene of action.

For that was what it was, a scene of action, or perhaps a hive of activity. In one room a Home Guard armourer was busy overhauling rifles and machine-guns. In another an unarmed combat expert was teaching the novices how to make others fall and also how to fall themselves. The mattress showed signs of constant use for this purpose. In the largest classroom fifty or sixty men in uniform were doing arms drill, and doing it with a click; in a small one a machine-gun team were stripping and assembling their weapon; while around a full-size billiard-table in another a squad of recruits in civvies were learning their first lessons under a patient but strict N.C.O.

I was introduced to officers and N.C.O.'s, and made free of the whole place, being permitted to ask, as my friend put it, " as many dam' silly questions as you like. We're used to 'em." So I spent a happy hour doing just that, and came to the conclusion that there was one marked difference between a city Home Guard and a village one. The latter are unashamed irregulars; the former are soldiers, or, shall I say, the pre-war territorials come to life.

That difference is mainly on account of numbers and premises. In town both are automatically available, especially in a blitzed town, where the men are really spiteful, and many schools and other premises are empty. Thus, in addition to the training carried on in these premises,

I found a social club in full swing. Besides the billiard-table there were a wet and a dry canteen and facilities for other amusements. In a village, although numbers are small, indoor training is almost invariably cramped for room, and the social side must depend mainly on the good offices of the landlord of the Wheatsheaf or the Bell.

But up here in town I found the same enthusiasm and pride in the Home Guard. When training was over that evening I talked with all and sundry, and this is the sort of thing I heard.

" Oh yes. Our district is all connected by telephone. Not the public sort, but by private lines of our own, put in by ourselves on Sundays and evenings. True, the municipal authorities, the police, and the public utility companies did everything to enable us to do it."

" Where did you get the wire ? " I asked.

They grinned.

" Oh, we indented for it, and they sent some, and the rest just happened."

I had sense enough not to inquire further. Is not the true history of the Home Guard's maintenance and equipment written clearly in the canteen conversation of every unit ?

Again, when I asked whether they were losing many of their younger men through their being called up into the regular forces, I obtained this.

" Yes, but our young men get a stripe in the army in next to no time. You see, they know their drill."

In one connexion these London Home Guards frankly envied the rural ones.

" We have to do most of our training indoors," they said to me. " You can get outside with your chaps any fine Sunday. Still, we do have a bit of fun in the parks sometimes."

But their greatest pride was that in spite of losing young

men to the regular Services, after a year and a half their numbers were steadily rising, and the first-joined members were still keen.

" Look," said the O.C., showing me the strength returns. " And look again at this. The other Sunday I asked for a minimum of two hundred men for an exercise, and how many turned up ? Two hundred and sixty-five."

That spoke volumes for a volunteer force, which at that date was subject to no compulsory attendances whatever.

A few weeks after this informal visit to North London I spent a day in Kent. This was a more formal visit, as I was taken in tow by, thanks be, a very kindly Staff officer. He asked what I most wanted to see, and I suggested that a coastal Home Guard unit would be most interesting to a member of an inland one, and especially one that had been shot over. He informed me that all Kent had been shot over and bombed over, and parts of it shelled from France, but that he would take me to the Isle of Thanet.

We arrived there by car one cold Sunday morning to find the towns and countryside under snow. Now, while snow beautifies the countryside it does the reverse for towns. But even without snow and with a shining sun Thanet would have been depressing, for of its peace-time population of some sixteen thousand people only some three thousand remained. Consequently I saw very few women and children, but many bombed or deserted houses. To these two depressing features, plus snow and a cold wind, I added a memory of Thanet in peace-time, and the result was the grimmest picture ever.

I had read of the repeated enemy bombing raids on this county. I knew that Kent had given up many hundreds of acres of good fat farming land for war purposes. I recognized that no other county was quite so much in the actual front line of battle. There was no doubt that in this war Kent had suffered hardly. But it was, I know, those hundreds of deserted houses in Thanet that brought this home to me so distinctly.

Most of them were little houses, and not very good houses at that—in fact, many might be described as being rather of the bandbox type. Even before this war they had little dignity in themselves, but then they did boast the wonderful dignity of being homes—homes of free people living in no fear of physical danger. Then they housed a family; then there were children playing in the little gardens. Now those houses were empty, undignified shells of homes. In due time their snow-covered gardens would show June roses blooming above a riot of weeds. Now their *raison d'être* had disappeared completely, and the sight of such desolation made me shiver.

Even so the Thanet Home Guard was busy that Sunday morning, having staged all sorts of small exercises and demonstrations on our behalf. I saw a truck driven over the snow, and a spigot mortar unloaded and in action in less than a minute. I saw men of all ages playing their respective parts, seemingly heedless of the snow and a biting wind. And I looked from the cliffs over a leaden sea, and marvelled aloud.

" You have us beaten," I confessed to the O.C. " At home on a day like this we should cancel outdoor training on the grounds that it is silly to have a lot of middle-aged men knocked up with colds."

" Don't blame you," he replied. " But you haven't quite got this Kent thing. Many of my men have had their wives and children killed or injured by bombs, have lost their houses, businesses, and pre-war jobs by the same means. They're sticking here in Thanet until they get a chance to hit back, and they'll train for that in spite of snow, hail, or anything."

Incidentally, I think it was Thanet that was primarily responsible for the institution of a subsistence allowance being paid to the Home Guard. So many people had left this district, and, its pre-war business of catering for seaside visitors having disappeared, it had soon become difficult to find employment for many of the men still remaining. But, as Thanet was already in the forefront of the battle and would be most likely to get the first bump of an invasion, a strong Home Guard there was essential. To put the men into a Home Defence battalion would not solve the problem, because the terms of such enlistment would render them liable to be moved to any spot in Britain. So a subsistence allowance of eighteenpence per head for continuous duty of over five hours and three shillings for over ten hours was instituted. This enabled the Thanet men whose civilian earnings had dwindled considerably to carry on, as around that dangerous coast-line they put in many hours on Home Guard duty.

One of the best examples of the quality of the Home Guard in that district was an exhibition of firing live grenades from a projector. My officer guide and I sploshed through the snow to where a middle-aged subaltern was in charge of the demonstration, with two young lads of perhaps seventeen as gunners.

He took a grenade from the box, inserted the detonator, and handed it to one of the lads. The boy inserted it into the projector hind-part before, carefully pulled out the pin, put in the charge, and slammed the breech-block home. As he fired we watched the grenade fly in a beautiful lob slap on to the target, an old motor-lorry a hundred and fifty yards distant, and explode according to plan.

Three times was this repeated successfully, but the fourth grenade failed to explode.

" Ah," said the Staff officer. " How are you going to deal with that ? Got your demolition materials ? "

" No, sir. But, as you well know, we've been indenting for 'em for months."

F

" Yes, of course. Supplies are short. Well, you'll have to get in touch with some regulars. Where is the nearest engineer unit ? "

" Oh, I can deal with this job all right, sir."

" How ? If you haven't got the right materials ? "

" Well, sir, I've got a bit of stick."

At this point my manners forsook me, and I chuckled aloud. However, he produced his piece of stick, which had a short screw at one end that would fit the gas check hole in the rear of a grenade.

He then casually took another grenade from the box, inserted a detonator, and then screwed this live grenade on to his stick.

" Humph ! " said the Staff officer. " And what are you going to do now ? "

" Well, you see, sir, I've got an elastic band." Here I chortled once more, as from a pocket in his battle-dress he produced one.

" But I still don't see—— "

" Well, sir, I'm going down there to find the unexploded grenade, shall put it side of this one, and put this band round both of them. Then I shall fix the stick firmly, tie a string to the pin of the live one, and pull it out from cover."

" That is a very expensive way of dealing with a blind grenade."

" Maybe, sir, but you show me a better one, when you don't send the proper materials."

Then came the amazing thing. Nonchalantly the lieutenant and the two lads strolled towards the target, and soon I could see them pawing in the snow under that lorry in search of the unexploded grenade. After a few moments they found it, casually wondered aloud why it had not exploded—I'm not certain they didn't shake it— in unhurried fashion clipped it to the live one on the stick, fixed the string, and in due course blew up the two grenades together. Against all rules may be ; damn' silly may be ; reckless certainly ; but never have I been prouder of the force of which I was a member. With the materials available they dealt with the situation successfully, and it was evident that in like fashion they would deal successfully with any situation that came along.

In fact, self-help seems to have been the Thanet Home Guard's motto from the word go. During this visit I was told many tales to illustrate their methods. Of a Home Guard battalion who manned the cliffs during those fateful early days—nine hundred men, the majority untrained, and armed with but one rifle for every ten men. Of the landing of tired soldiers from Dunkirk beach at the pleasure steamers' pier below them as they anxiously watched the sea between Kent and the French coast. Of rifles and ammunition, landed there by the same means, that somehow found its way into the hands of the Home Guard on the cliffs above. The details of how this happened cannot be disclosed until after the war, but no one can censure those responsible. Why ? Simply because during that dangerous period of the evacuation from Dunkirk and for some weeks afterwards those Thanet Home Guards had been informed by higher military authorities in Kent that they must consider themselves to be the bait for the invader. So the bait broke all the rules and equipped itself to do the biting.

Until now this chapter has dealt with the impressions of the visitor. For the other side of the picture, those of the visitee, I must visit Sedgebury Wallop once again. Towards the tail end of the summer of 1941 Walter Pocock had become a platoon officer. In his view this was a mistake, and he had said as much to his superior officers, pointing out that his friend, Tom Butler, should have been the man to receive this promotion. However, neither they nor Tom agreed with him, and so, proudly yet shamefacedly, he put up one pip, remarking, " Now I'm properly labelled as what I look like and feel like—a grandfather in rompers."

A week or two after his promotion a platoon officer from a neighbouring platoon called on him with the news that the powers above had suggested that the two of them should run a small demonstration in Sedgebury Wallop.

" You see, Walter, I've just been to a street-fighting demonstration, and I've been asked to repeat it in this battalion. The old man suggested Wallop main street as a suitable place and you as my companion in crime. We've got to stage the show one Sunday, and the rest of the battalion will come as spectators—including generals and one hell of a hoo-ha."

" Hum ! Since when have I been considered either a military expert or a film producer ? "

" Search me, but honestly, Walter, it isn't a bad story. Have a look."

He handed over the official typewritten narrative, and lit his pipe, while his friend read it.

The story described the attack on a Home Guard unit by a small force of enemy parachute troops, and went something like this. Action stations had been given several days before, but nothing had happened in the district, and the local Home Guard had become rather bored with the whole business. A footsore civilian carrying a suitcase approaches the sentry at the traffic barrier in a railway arch on the outskirts of the village street. He informs the sentry that all the trains had stopped twenty miles up the line, and that he had been forced to walk to his destination, his sister's house at number six.

The sentry looks at his identity card, and after some five minutes' chat passes him through the block, pointing out that number six is some twenty yards farther down the street, just past some riflemen posted behind a hedge. The riflemen, unsoldierly scallywags, come out to chat with him, and in conversation inform him that they have two Lewis guns, tell him where their men are posted, and every detail of the defence. The sentry turns round to join in this conversation, yelling that the newcomer's identity card is O.K.

While this is going on and the sentry's back is towards his post a bunch of enemy dash over the railway embankment, unseen by the defenders. The civilian goes into number six, opens his bag, takes out a tommy-gun, fits it together, and then comes out. From the cover of the porch of number six he shoots the sentry and three of the four riflemen. The fourth runs round the block of houses to be killed by the enemy, who are now in the first house. A bomber on the railway embankment now stands up to throw, and the fifth columnist shoots him also. An enemy machine-gun then opens up from the top of the railway embankment, killing several Home Guards farther down the street, for by now the whole defence has waked up to the fact that it is being attacked. Before they can do much, being kept under cover by the machine-gun, the main force of enemy rush the archway, and join their companions and the fifth columnist under cover in the first house.

Having accomplished this, they then proceed to drive out the women and children in the other houses, and to use them as a screen as they advance down the street. In this way they scupper the main defence force, and clear the whole block ready for their mechanized vehicles to follow. During this main attack one or two little children are shot, whereupon a civilian, the man who couldn't be bothered to join the Home Guard, rushes out with a shot-gun, and is immediately shot by the enemy. For demonstration purposes all this is to take place on one side of the street only, in order that spectators can line the opposite side.

" Well," said Second Lieutenant Walker, as Walter came to the end of this narrative, " what d'you think of it ? "

" A good story, Bill. One that might easily happen."

" Then you'll play, and help me stage it in Wallop ? "

" Like hell I will. What ? Stage a show that illustrates that the Home Guard doesn't know the first thing about its job after more than a year's training ? Bill, you find another mug."

" But, Walter, they staged it at So-and-so, and everybody reckoned it a first-class show."

" Let 'em. Yours truly won't touch it unless it's done both ways."

" How d'you mean ? "

" Well, show a successful attack as this describes. Then show a successful defence, the same attack scuppered on the same ground by a Home Guard that has tried to learn its job."

" Yes, but I've asked all over the place, and none of the bigwigs will give me a script of a successful defence."

" Bigwigs be sugared. This is just the sort of little job that the average Home Guard platoon may have to tackle. Why can't we work out a successful defence ? "

" Too big a risk, Walter. We'll have five hundred spectators of all ranks as critics."

" Well, what of it ? Let 'em criticize. Here, wait till I ring up Tom Butler."

When Tom came, although the old soldier in him realized the risk his friends would run in working out a successful defence on their own, he was eager to share in it ; so the three of them worked far into the night to formulate a plan that would counter every phase of the attack. Here is how the discussion went.

" You asked for the job, Walter," said Tom, " so you give us a start."

Walter Pocock grinned, scratched his bald head, and said, " All right, little man, here goes. First thing we'll have a cyclist scout out well forward on every approach. Outer barrier open with sentry as before, but that sentry covered by mate in cottage opposite. Apart from the two sentries and the scouts the main force will be at rest at headquarters, with a machine-gun team ready to move out on the jump."

" So that," chuckled Tom, " the C.O., in this case Lieutenant Pocock, can sleep at peace knowing that no enemy are within two miles of his boundaries. Carry on, Hitler."

" Right. First intimation of attack will be arrival of cyclist scout reporting enemy in neighbourhood. Outer block immediately closed with both sentries under cover, and messages sent to neighbouring platoons and company H.Q. C.O. posts men. One bomber on embankment with orders to lie doggo until the right moment. Four riflemen behind hedge as before, but L.M.G. teams posted out on flanks. Useless having 'em firing straight up the street. Squad sent to turn out all civilians in houses in front of main road block. This done the squad rejoins main force under cover but on their toes."

" Excellent, Walter," said Tom. " And here's an idea. Have one ex-soldier civilian refuse to turn out, saying that he was fighting years before the Home Guard began playing at it. So the Home Guard hustles him out at the point of the bayonet. Old Simmons would play that part fine. Now then, the post is ready, Bill. Bring on your fifth columnist."

" Yes, and I'm getting the wheeze. He advances to the outer barrier as before, and is halted and questioned by concealed sentry in house opposite. Same tale of halted trains and his sister in number six, and then—— ? "

" Concealed sentry then tells him to halt until he comes out to check his identity card," said Tom. " This is done with fifth columnist on far side of barrier and sentry inside it. Card seems all in order, but sentry asks what he has in his bag."

" He replies that he has his night things and a present for his sister's kiddies," suggested Bill Walter.

" Which ain't good enough for a Wallop sentry, who insists that he must see the contents of the bag before he permits the man to pass the barrier," said Walter.

" Whereupon, seeing the game's up, the fifth columnist pulls revolver, and—— "

" Is shot dead by sentry's mate in house opposite. Sentry hooks bag under the barrier to examine it, and—— "

" Is shot dead by small squad of attackers as they cross railway embankment," cut in Butler. " Bli' me, it's as good as a play. Your turn, Walter."

" Wallop L.M.G. on flank opens up, and accounts for that squad, and your blooming attack has been scuppered from the word go."

" Good enough, Walter," chortled Tom. " Rommel has nothing on us."

" Wait a bit," laughed Bill Walker. " There's still the main attack to deal with. Although their plan has obviously gone wrong, this block must be cleared, so they rush the railway arch under cover of smoke."

" And cop it proper," countered Tom Butler. " You've forgotten our bomber. He's been lying doggo all this time. He will, too, for I've spent months knocking that into his fool head. He flips a couple of grenades into your attack from side of the archway, making a proper mess."

" Yes, I'll grant that, but enough get through to scupper the four riflemen, and gain the cover of the first house in the block behind them. From there they launch an attack on the main block farther down the street."

" But there are no civilians in the houses to use as a screen and no time to filter down over roofs. So they move

as quickly as possible down the side, taking cover under
porches and such like."

"Good enough. But what about your civilian with a
shot-gun? Doesn't he play in this act?" inquired Walter.

"Sure he does," said Tom. "The fool hid himself
when the Home Guard turned out the women and kids.
Now he comes out to do or die."

"And is shot by the Wallop Home Guard the moment
he appears," suggested Walter. "You see, they've already
had trouble with the fifth columnist civilian, and they ain't
takin' any chances. So any civvy with arms in his hands
gets it."

"Hooray!" chortled Tom. "That'll be the high spot
of the show. Then the enemy attack rushes past his body,
and is caught in a cross-fire at the next lane from flanking
L.M.G.'s and riflemen, the survivors surrendering to the
Home Guard."

"And that," murmured Bill Walker, "will be that."

"Not quite," said Tom. "Remember, we shall have laid
ourselves open to criticism, so let's tidy up the end properly."

"How so, Tom?" asked Walter.

"Well, that may be the end of a demonstration, but in
real warfare it wouldn't be the end. The first thing the
Wallop C.O. must do is to order scouts out forward, replace
the dead sentry, and make ready for a second attack."

In this fashion they doped out their scheme for a successful
defence, and after polishing it for several days they submitted
it to their superior officers. These commended it in the
main, suggested one or two improvements, and in due
course came along to help with the rehearsals.

Two Sundays later the demonstration was given before a
large crowd of Home Guard and regulars with marked
success. In fact, there was only one slip. Somehow or
other the forward scout got the signal to report three
minutes before he should have done, with the result that the

defence had to meet a real surprise attack. Which was a great improvement, for even so the plan worked out well, earning much praise and only two criticisms. One of these came from the general who was in charge of the whole area. " Where," he demanded of the battalion commander, " did these blighters get hold of all that blank and bombs ? "

A respectful reply suggested that it would be best not to inquire details.

" I see," chuckled the great man. " But one thing I must know. How do they make a .300 L.M.G. work like that ? There's no blank in this country for a .300 machine-gun."

" That, sir," came the reply, " was the Wallop special. Four-ten shot cartridge-cases cut down and loaded with black powder, and used in a .45 revolver to imitate bursts of machine-gun fire."

And then he made his comment. " But I never knew," he murmured, " that I was commanding a troupe of actors."

Granted it was only a very small and amateurish show, but it did point out two things. Firstly, that the Home Guard was too proud to depict itself only in the rôle of defeat ; and secondly, that it was game enough to risk its own plan being laughed at by the experts.

But truth must be told—there was a fly in the ointment that morning. After the show was over the local pub ran dry of beer far too soon.

CHAPTER 7

Intensive Training

FIFTEEN hundred thousand men who were determined to learn soldiering in their spare time required not only arms and equipment, but also training. But where were the instructors ? The regular army had none to spare, so Home Guard instructors had to be provided from the Home Guard itself. Ex-soldier officers and N.C.O.'s badly needed refresher courses and new training in modern warfare, while those Home Guard leaders who possessed no military experience needed tuition in every detail of their new job.

It was obvious that training-schools for instructors were badly needed, but during that hectic period immediately after Dunkirk the War Office had its hands more than full, so in the beginning most of these training-schools were started by amateurs. These schools were soon recognized and helped by the War Office, and in some cases were subsequently taken over as official training-schools.

Not until late 1941 could I find time to attend any of them, but in December of that year I met and lunched with John Langdon-Davies in London, and was invited by him to come down to his Fieldcraft School at Burwash, in Sussex, on the following Friday for a week-end course. From what I have been able to find out about the early history of this school it began by Mr Langdon-Davies, backed by the *Sunday Pictorial*, instructing the local Home Guard near his house, Bowman's, with the idea of subsequently using them as instructors to Home Guard visitors from a distance.

It was a success from the word go. The local Home Guard played up nobly. The local baker became quartermaster-sergeant, a carpenter and a mechanic became corporals, and with Mr Langdon-Davies as Commandant, these first instructed fifty fairly local students. Afterwards these came in batches of eight each week-end to act as demonstrators to students from a distance. These initiates then went away to spread the light in their own platoons. By the time I went to Burwash the school had become widely known, and in December 1941 it became an official training-school of the South-eastern Command. In those early days what it lacked in necessary equipment it made up in volunteer work and enthusiasm, and soon became a shining example of the truth that money isn't everything. What I expected from it is immaterial; this is what I got.

It was cold that December, and when with some fifty Home Guards from all over England I paraded in the barn at Bowman's at ten o'clock that Friday night it was decidedly parky. The Commandant looked at us in the flickering light of one or two hurricane lanterns, and said, " I see. As usual every rank from private to lieutenant-colonel. Right ! From now until you leave on Monday morning there will be no ranks."

He then divided us into sections of twelve, and told each section to appoint a section leader, whose orders were to be obeyed without question. Very wisely each section chose for leader the man with the kindest face, and this hero was then ordered to appoint a latrine orderly, a food orderly, and a bedding orderly.

The Commandant then explained that the main idea of this week-end course was to instruct us how to live and fight and eat and sleep always under fire from the enemy. During every moment we must imagine that the village of Burwash, about half a mile away from Bowman's, was in the hands of the enemy, who had machine-guns trained on our camp. Therefore, during daylight, we must never show ourselves, even if this meant crawling about in the Sussex clay. He hoped that we had brought denim uniforms for this purpose, as by Sunday night our clothes would be fairly muddy. Moreover, shaving was against the rules. As far as possible we were to live under active service conditions, and so learn how to be able to look after our own men at home under those conditions if the need arose. Then, at about 2300 hours the students went to bed on straw in barns, lofts, and outhouses.

Next morning rations for the day—bully beef, tea, potatoes, and bread—were drawn from the quartermaster-sergeant, and we settled down to work. The students that week-end were all sorts—landowners, farmers, farm labourers, Kent miners who had given up several pounds of wages to take the course, factory owners, factory hands, professional men, retail traders—a comprehensive cross-section of male civilian life in Britain.

First we paraded for arms inspection, each man having been instructed to bring a rifle and some ball ammunition and to carry it during all operations and training. This was done on the grounds that any Home Guard worth his salt, and especially one who aspired to the rôle of instructing his fellows, should be able to handle weapons at all times with complete safety. Thereafter we attended lectures in the big barn, and engaged in outdoor exercises and training.

The rule that at all times we must behave as though under fire from Burwash seemed at first to be rather an unnecessary joke, but soon it became an accepted part of our lives. To obey it properly, even if one wanted merely to cross the narrow gap between the barn and an outhouse, one must crawl in the mud. Having dirtied oneself properly one then saw to it that everybody else played the game, and by nightfall on the first day we looked a sorry lot of scare-crows. Truly, stout middle age crawling on its belly to procure a light for a cigarette presented a weird spectacle.

In and around that isolated steading of Bowman's Farm we learned all sorts of things : how to master our equipment instead of being a slave to it ; what parts of it showed up at a distance, and how best to conceal or camouflage them ; that our faces showed up distinctly, and that green blanco plus a stiff stubble was the best concealing agent, the former also being used on our hands.

We learned how to bivouac in face of the enemy, and how to make a satisfactory sleeping-tent with two ground sheets, a length of binder twine, and a few wooden pegs. We were instructed in the principles of camp hygiene—in other words, shown that it was safer to live like cats rather than like dogs ; how to camouflage the steel helmet, how to make and use a sniper's suit, and how to use our eyes ; how to send and how not to send messages under all sorts of conditions ; how to crawl quickly with a rifle ready to hand. We experienced a vivid hour of unarmed combat under the supervision of army instructors. We learned how to move silently and invisibly over all sorts of country, and how to live on minimum army rations cooked by ourselves.

We also learned how to move silently under cover on all types of surfaces from brickbats to Sussex clay and brambles. The procedure was for half the students to essay the stalking course, while the other half criticized their methods and noted their mistakes from a suitable distance. Afterwards the rôles were reversed.

This stalking course was my undoing. Having first been an observer, when I subsequently found myself faced with a length of sliminess guarded by cover only a bare foot in height I decided to rush it. I afterwards learned that for middle age of my girth this was the best method. Anyway, realizing that the flat crawl was beyond me, from a crouched position I ran that ten-feet gap in the high cover at speed, slipped, went for six, and pitched on a stone. I did not break any ribs ; but, as my hunter had planted his foot on that particular spot some three years before, I was obliged to laugh carefully for the remainder of that course and for several weeks afterwards.

A fair description of that course was that it was tough but great fun. The water-supply was by well and bucket, the lighting by oil hurricane lanterns. The latter was a great blessing, as it meant that after dark training and lectures must stop, and this enabled a gang of unshaven toughs to visit the pub at Burwash in the evenings, and drown some of their aches and pains in beer.

But I came away firmly convinced that such training was very necessary for the average Home Guard. It stirred his imagination, and enabled him to picture possible war conditions and how best to work under them. In many ways I was reminded of my life in a shanty in North-west Manitoba some thirty years before. Neither before nor since had I been so cold and hungry, or so possessed of the zest for living and working.

Christmas over, in early January 1942 I did an intensive week's training at a school in the country. Here, although there was some fieldcraft work, the emphasis was on weapon training. Again, this was a school that had been started by an enthusiastic amateur. It began at Osterley Park under Mr Tom Wintringham in July 1940, being financed by Mr Edward Hulton with the object of training Home Guards to make the best use of the few weapons then available. In September of that year it was taken over by the War Office, and in October moved to its present site.

That week, and it was still bitterly cold, was one of intensive training with a vengeance—breakfast at 0745 hours, and thereafter steady work all day with short breaks for lunch and tea, the last lecture finishing sometimes at 2100 hours. At the end of it I, and I think most of the members of that course, were suffering badly from mental indigestion. One thing, however, was especially pleasing to most of us. We learned a tremendous lot that we did not know, but we were pleased to discover also that in our own amateurish ways at home during the previous eighteen months we had learned quite a lot that was worth while.

Realizing my limitations in all military matters, I was determined to be as inconspicuous as possible. Alas! It was a case of man proposes, but the sergeant-major disposes. After breakfast on the Monday we all met on the gravel outside the house waiting for the how and why of the initial parade. Suddenly down the path from the orderly room marched five men and the sergeant-major.

" Halt! Fall out the drummer," was barked into the still air of a frosty morning.

Any old student will remember the word of command and the scene.

Having spaced his four markers the great man then ordered the unsoldierly rabble on the gravel to fall in in two ranks. We did this more or less to his satisfaction, and I carefully hid myself in the rear rank lest worse befall. It did. The numbering of the front rank showed seventy-two men on parade.

" Right! Four platoons each of eighteen men. Numbers nine, eighteen, twenty-seven, and thirty-six in the rear rank will automatically become platoon sergeants for the week, and be responsible for their platoons."

And I was number nine!

However, I managed to get by, but during the week that followed from dawn till long after dark neither I nor any of my companions had a minute in which to think, worry, or wonder. Instead we were continuously absorbing useful information. We learned the ins and outs and tricks of every weapon already issued to the Home Guard, and also of those soon to be issued—bombs of every type, sub-artillery, grenades, flame-throwers and fougasses, rifles, and even shot-guns. Moreover, we fired or saw fired every weapon and thus learned its effect. In addition, the tactical use of every weapon was explained. Some idea of the work of this school can be gathered from the number of students that it turned out as Home Guard instructors. By the end of 1941 nearly five thousand had been passed through.

The lecturers ranged from regular officers to Home Guards and civilians, and all seemed to have discarded the regulation attitude to our problems, and talked to us in language possibly unfit for little boys but very suitable for Home Guards. There was the Commandant, Lieutenant-Colonel Pollock, who fairly doted on sub-artillery, and lecturers who had either learned something of modern war in Spain, were experts in dirty tricks or thuggery, or apparently slept each night from choice with live bombs as bedfellows, and all sorts.

On the last night of the course an officer from the Home Guard Directorate came down to dine, and subsequently to receive grouses and suggestions from enthusiasts in good measure. There were also the sergeant-major, his four markers, and the drummer. Together they gave us a great week, and sent us all back to our platoons fairly bursting with new information and new tricks to try out at home.

In addition to these weekly courses the school does some invaluable work by sending out travelling wings all over the country. In this connexion it can be likened to a parent ship or aircraft-carrier, and its travelling wings to either submarines or aircraft. In this way the school supplies for the Home Guard what Mr Fortune would describe as " a felt want."

One of the handicaps of the work of permanent schools is that so many of the men who form the backbone of the Home Guard cannot attend them. They are first and foremost civilians, who each month find increasing difficulties to face in order to do their civilian jobs properly. The wealthy man, the retired man, and even the professional man can somehow take a week off to attend a permanent school ; but in most cases the farmer, the farm foreman, the village

G

shopkeeper, the local garage proprietor and his best mechanic, the house-thatcher, the local builder, and all those country-men who by their own merit have attained some little position in the countryside cannot manage this. The ties and responsibilities of their civilian jobs will not permit, and I have a notion that the same state of things obtains also in town Home Guard units. But such men can and are only too eager to take a week-end at a travelling school in their district, and I know that all who have done this have learned a lot of useful knowledge and appreciated the opportunity of doing so.

One feature of this intensive training, either at permanent schools or in travelling wings, is its unorthodox character. Those of us at the school who had expected unimaginative officialism from hide-bound army lecturers were agreeably surprised to find exactly the reverse. There was no attempt to mould us to the regulation pattern, or to turn us into second- or third-rate soldiers. Instead, it was evident that the object was to develop any flair for improvisation, to encourage individualism, and to produce first-class irregulars or even rural bandits.

A few weeks after my return from the course news came that the Home Guard was soon to receive a general issue of spigot mortars. First reports of this weapon gave it a tricky character, and one or two accidents had demonstrated that it was not a safe toy for novices. Even so, there was no doubt that, properly handled, it would provide the Home Guard with its first piece of sub-artillery capable of hitting really hard, of knocking out a tank, and even of turning enemy out of buildings. But trained instructors were considered essential ; so, as I had seen something of this weapon in use, my Company Commander suggested that I should be the sacrifice, and ordered me to proceed forth-with to yet another school for a five-day course of intensive training with this mortar.

With regard to the personal comfort of students a fair comparison of the three training-schools that I have attended would be to say that the first was tough with short hours, the second comfortable with long hours, and the third luxurious but with the strictest training possible. To put it another way, the first possessed no amenities, the second was an awkward country house in process of alteration, while the third accommodated its students, both Home Guards and regulars, commissioned and non-commissioned, in the luxurious quarters of numerous seaside hotels. In this way the third school could accommodate and train hundreds of students at the same time. There were specialist courses in every weapon, comprehensive training courses for Home Guards, tough courses for would-be commando troops, and all sorts.

My companions on the spigot-mortar course were a mixed bunch of forty, who were handed over to two staff sergeants for instruction. This meant that each instructor took a class of twenty, a very curious mixture. For instance, in my class there were two regular officers, three Home Guard officers, and a regular sergeant-major, the remainder being made up of regular and Home Guard N.C.O.'s in equal proportions. For five days our instructor wrought with us faithfully, and never once did he lose control of that difficult mixture ; never once was he unfair to any section of it ; and by the end of the fifth day he had taught us the tricks of that mortar and its powerful bombs backward, forward, and sideways. It was a triumph of tact, discipline, and expert knowledge.

One of the great difficulties most students from these training-schools found on their return to their units was that at least two-thirds of their audience possessed no previous experience of actual warfare. It was easy to pass on the information concerning the mechanism of new weapons and ammunition, but the explanation of their tactical rôle and actual effect on active service was another matter. It was almost impossible for civilians like myself to realize that war, even minor war in our own village, would mean battle, murder, sudden death, and all sorts of ruthless happenings that were undreamed of in our philosophy. As a civilian instructor I found this difficulty well-nigh insurmountable.

For instance, one evening after doing my best to explain how a certain weapon might operate in our own position I invited questions.

" Supposing we fire that sort of bomb at a tank at our block and miss the tank, that bomb will go all down the village street. Won't that be rather awkward ? "

Admitting that I had no experience of it, I replied that I had always been given to understand that war was, not rather awkward, but bloody awkward, with the emphasis on the adjective. I also pointed out that when we were engaged in such capers it was unlikely that the civil population would be meandering up the street to church.

" I can see that we might very well knock out one tank with this weapon, but supposing there are several tanks, what will happen to the team operating it ? "

To that I was forced to reply that the second tank would most likely swivel its gun and knock out our weapon and its team. But I suggested that if three Home Guards had been skilful enough to knock out an expensive enemy tank with such a cheap weapon, the loss of both weapon and team would be much less than the gain achieved by them. Frankly, I was rather guessing in these replies, but, thanks be, the old soldiers in the platoon backed up a green-horn. They had been there, and they knew.

However, there is no doubt that the work of the various training-schools did provide the Home Guard all over Britain with amateur instructors capable of giving much useful training to their units, and that as a result the majority of the Home Guard to-day do know how to use and care for their weapons, and something of their tactical rôle in the event of enemy invasion. Moreover, with knowledge comes pride. Now that war restrictions and war work have made travelling almost impossible, every village community is forced back on itself for entertainment and competition during its leisure hours. Football and cricket have disappeared, the cinema is difficult to reach, and so Home Guard competitions must fill the gaps. These take place in the platoon, against neighbouring platoons, and sometimes throughout a battalion.

For instance, during the autumn of 1941 the Sedgebury Wallop platoon received news that in the near future there was to be a shooting competition, in order to find out the crack platoon of the Wessex battalion. Walter Pocock passed on this advance information to a crowded indoor miniature rifle-range one evening.

" We practise hard to select the best team. Then we shoot it out on a miniature range between the other platoons in the company. Then the winners go to camp one Sunday to shoot it out with the other winning platoons in the battalion at two hundred yards with Service rifles."

" Application or snap, Walter ? " inquired Tom Butler.

" Both. But there's one big snag. All shooting—miniature, long-range, application, and snap—has to be done in full kit and wearing respirators. So, my sons, if you want to win this you must do all your miniature firing in respirators from now on."

Which they did, slowly but surely improving, and in a few weeks found out the men who were least handicapped by the respirator. In due course they became the representatives of the company in the competition proper, and then turned their attention to long-range. In the beginning there were plenty of good marksmen at application, but not many who could even hit a target that popped up in different places for four seconds only at a range of two hundred yards.

At this game the respirator was a big handicap, especially to the man who perspired easily. Eventually, the best eight were sorted out, those who failed to qualify taking their disappointment in good humour, and volunteering as markers.

When the great day came the application test showed the Wallop team to occupy third place, but only a few points behind the leaders. But at the snap-shooting they fairly ran away from the others, and came out easy winners, to their great delight, especially as a team from the provincial town of Yarborough had been hot favourites. When it was all over, the team asked Walter if the result of their triumph could be sent to the local paper. Not knowing the correct military etiquette, and realizing that because of this he had put his foot in it more than once, Walter asked the adjutant of the battalion for a ruling.

" I don't quite know," came the reply. " It could be done, I suppose, but is it really necessary ? "

Here Shep Yates, the Wallop sergeant who had captained the team, struck in. " If Yarborough had won it, sir, 'twould ha' bin in every paper in England."

At this the adjutant laughed aloud, and promised to do the needful, subsequently spending the remainder of his Sunday in producing a comprehensive report of the competition.

As can be imagined, when the Wallop team arrived home the beer flowed in the Wheatsheaf, and Shep Yates pointed out that one good shot who had been forced to play the rôle of marker because of his inability to cope with a respirator for snap-shooting was the life and soul of the party.

" Fred'll be late for dinner to-day, sir," he remarked to Walter. " When I picked him up this morning his wife asked whether he would be home in time for dinner, and this is what he said : ' If Wallop loses I shan't want any dinner, and if Wallop wins I shan't care when I come home '."

Walter chuckled. There was no doubt about it—the Home Guard had restored village pride.

CHAPTER 8

Scots Wha Hae

DURING war-time life for all civilians, and especially for Home Guard civilians, is indeed a busy business. Anyway, in my own case it has been far too busy, and travelling far too difficult to enable me to make a comprehensive tour of the country and visit every type of Home Guard unit. Therefore, although I am aware of the mounted Home Guards in moorland country, of water-borne Home Guards in lakeland districts, and of many others that do not conform to the general pattern, I have been able to give intimate details only of the Home Guards in the south of England. But, apart from differences in transport, the same spirit, methods, and activities are to be found in every Home Guard battalion throughout the whole country.

However, when I said as much to my friend, Alexander Keith, during a hurried forty-eight-hour stay in Aberdeen during the summer of 1942, he argued that the Scottish Home Guard merited a chapter on its own. I agreed, but pleaded that I had neither the time to gather the necessary material, the ability to do justice to Scotland, nor a pen capable of getting the true Caledonian flavour on to paper. Even so, he demanded a Scottish chapter, and practically threatened to invade England with his Aberdonian Home Guards if this were not included. My only possible counter-attack was to insist that he must send me the necessary material. Here it is, unabridged.

The general outline of the history of the Home Guard in Scotland is very similar to that of the Home Guard in England and Wales. There was the same rush to join,

in city and country district, when the Local Defence
Volunteers were formed. There was the same long process
of sorting out and settling down, the same (or perhaps more
protracted) wait for arms and equipment. As regards
details, in development of the organization and particularly
in its training and in its approach to its peculiar problems,
there are substantial differences. These arise partly out of
the national characteristics of the two peoples, and partly
out of the peculiar conditions that govern the schemes of
defence of the two countries. For instance, the famous
call-out in September 1940 had to be postponed until 1000
hours the following morning for one isolated unit in Scotland
whose telephone system was suspended during the hours of
darkness. No contact being possible by that means, and
there being no other method of communication, authority
had to make the best of a bad job and leave the message to go
through when facilities for transmitting it became available.

It is probably not desirable that some of these differences
and distinctions should be gone into, although they are
obvious enough. One of them, however, arising out of the
more scattered distribution of the population in Scotland,
combined in certain areas with the difficult nature of the
country, has created in the sub-units—the companies,
platoons, and even the sections—of the Scottish Home
Guard a more independent tradition and a more pronounced
tendency to irregular and unconventional tactics. For
some unexplained, and perhaps inexplicable, reason the
word ' guerilla ' as applied to the Home Guard is frowned
upon by the authorities. In Scotland, to call a Home Guard
a ' guerilla ' is more likely to be appreciated than resented.
' Gorilla warfare ' would be the most apt description of the
sort of thing the Boche would encounter were he to attempt
to poke his nose into Scotland. During one exercise
between a fairly tough Scottish detachment and some city
units of the Home Guard the troops were so uncomprisingly

handled that they complained of the " roughness " of their opponents. As between units, especially neighbouring and therefore rival units, of the Home Guard it is often difficult for the participants in exercises to remember that they are performing an exercise, not dealing with an enemy. On the other hand, when units strangers to each other are co-operating, the liaison is none the less efficient for being informal. The presence of an N.C.O. is not necessary for the making of an arrangement to keep touch, and pass messages, and where necessary supply mutual covering fire.

The early days of jokes at the expense of Home Guards who did not know the business end of a rifle have passed. In at least one infantry training centre in Scotland it has been stated by the instructors, who have taken Home Guard as well as troops in hand, that the former know their weapons better than the latter. This is not astonishing, since about one-third of the Home Guard consists of men who a quarter of a century ago got a very thorough grounding in the use of weapons, and who might owe their lives to their proficiency. It is a common remark among unit commanders that when these old soldiers get the weapons and are confronted by a situation in a mimic battle they are never at a loss what to do, and their knowledge is diffused through the younger men in their section, platoon, or company. Cases have been recorded of small picquets and posts under ex-Servicemen holding up, with what would probably be regarded as quite inadequate weapons, a superior force, even supported by tanks, for a considerable period. The combination of youth and experience has given stamina to the whole, and for this reason Scotland has not taken kindly to the direction that sections should be graded according to the age of their members. In a high percentage of cases the toughs in any given units are not the young but the older men, between forty-two and fifty, who have seen active service. They may not be so fast on their feet, but they know what to do and know when to stick their toes in. One of the best instances of this steady determination occurred in a Scottish area on January 25, 1942, the wildest day for thirty-five years, when the snow seethed and swirled in the air like porridge stirred by some gigantic mixing-rod. A Commando demonstration had been arranged in a certain town for the Home Guard units within a six- or seven-mile radius. There was no transport that day by road or rail. The Commando failed to get through, but the Home Guards were all present, and returned as they had come, on foot.

The basic advantage the Home Guard possesses over a potential invader is its knowledge of its own locality. Sometimes this familiarity creates blind spots. In one exercise in the north of Scotland the scheme of things was that a force of Boches had captured the MacWhisky, the leader of the defending troops. He was in enemy hands at a point in the hills, when the Hun was expected to try to smuggle him through a cordon of Home Guards who had risen in their wrath to rescue their beloved chief. The Home Guards comprised shepherds, ghillies, and stalkers who knew every stone and heather bush in the countryside. Their commander took counsel with his men, and they decided that the enemy had only three practicable routes of escape. But the enemy, who were young lads from a training regiment, ignored all the conventions of mountaineering and, instead of contouring, fetched a direct compass course to their selected place of safety. They made it quite unnoticed by the ring of opponents surrounding them. True, the latter had neglected the elementary precaution of detailing scouts to keep an eye on the invaders, thinking that, as they knew where they were, there was no need to watch them. But the episode taught the lesson that you can never be too sure, and that the unconventional unexpectedly employed will often foil superior forces, skill, and knowledge.

A different result was obtained in another district by a Home Guard company commanded by a distinguished sportsman. This company was set an area covering several parishes to defend, and the lay-out of the exercise was that a brigade of troops, fully equipped with their transport, would play the Boche and occupy the area. The Home Guard commander had from the outset organized his diocese, civilian population as well as his own men. The people knew what to do. When the exercise opened, the inhabitants were warned that the invaders were coming, and reminded that when the Hun had come and settled in, they, as good Scots, were expected to bring in to a fixed rendezvous all the information possible about the strength and location of the enemy groups scattered throughout the district. The Home Guard organization there was based, outside the villages, on the large farms, each big farm being the headquarters of a squad with an N.C.O. The troops arrived and took up their quarters, parking their transport and selecting their own billets. The inhabitants proceeded on their lawful occasions, which, however, took unwonted numbers of them to the information rendezvous previously arranged. The particulars were conveyed in many ways, some so highly ingenious that they had better not be divulged while this war lasts.

Darkness fell. The brigadier was seated in his head-quarters in a room in the chief village of the occupied area. Suddenly on the table beneath his nose there appeared a large, muscular, and, it is said, not too clean hand. In the hand there was a 36 grenade. A very bucolic voice said, " Sorry "—the " sir " doesn't come easily or naturally in Lowland Scotland ; " sorry, but I doot ye're oot ! " Next morning the umpires went round the billets and parking places. On every billet and every vehicle there was a mark signifying that it and its contents had been dealt with. The umpires regretfully allowed that the invaders no longer existed. Yet not a sound had been heard that night.

Of course, the occasions in which the army has proved too much for the Home Guard are kept discreetly in the background. These occasions are more numerous, but not more spectacular, and there is no doubt that some of the exploits of the Home Guard early in its career were a tonic to the men. The first big exercise which brought the Home Guard in Scotland under the notice of the higher army authorities took place in a stretch of country where Montrose and Dundee had both shown their skill as guerilla leaders. The Home Guard commanders learned the lessons of those past masters. The arrangement was that a detachment of troops would march into the area, where the local Home Guard would play their allotted rôle of observing, harassing, and reporting. The invading column halted for the night and made themselves snug and sound, and, as they thought, safe. In the morning the divisional commander and his staff had disappeared, leaving not a trace of where or how they had gone. All day the troops searched, pushing up into the hills where sat the Home Guard, like so many hoodie-crows, watching with unblinking eyes, and with the general safety bestowed in a fastness of the wild upland country. The following night the Commander Royal Artillery was spirited away. The Home Guard, like the widow with her mite, had done what they could, and their prowess in this episode, perhaps elaborated and ornamented as it passed from mouth to mouth, occasioned much enthusiasm among the part-time soldiers.

That anecdote illustrates the acumen of a battalion commander. Another may be given to illustrate the ingenuity of a sergeant commanding a village section. In the exercise the hostile troops, under an officer, appeared in the village early one Sunday afternoon. The men debussed, and the officer took his N.C.O.'s along the village street to give them a sketch of the scheme and their orders. As they stood up a hand-cart came along, loaded with grass and with a scythe stuck in the load. The man who was pushing the hand-cart set it down beside the little group and went into the adjacent house. The cart was an inviting pivot for the conference, and by it the officer explained his plans. Then he and the N.C.O.'s went back to their men, preparatory to moving off to their appointed positions. They paid no attention to the man with the hand-cart, who came out of the house and made off with his burden. But he was veritably a man with a load of mischief. Underneath the grass was a Home Guard who had overheard the whole exposition, and who, as soon as the cart had got round the corner, emerged from his concealment and hastened to report to his sergeant. That worthy made his dispositions according to the welcome information thus received. The enemy took up their posts, but just as zero hour was reached each post was held up and put in the bag. There may have been a shade of sharp practice in thus anticipating zero hour, but Home Guard exercises in Scotland have usually been characterized by a surprising uncertainty which is a good deal more like what the real thing would be than any controlled development. The device adopted to get the vital information in this case is very interesting. Every Scottish schoolboy knows how, in the Wars of Independence, Roxburgh and Edinburgh Castle were taken, and the ruse of men concealed in a cart of hay with which a farmer, William Binnock, captured Linlithgow Castle, was probably remembered by the intelligent crofter who was the sergeant.

It must not be supposed, however, that the Home Guard in Scotland desire to score off the army from cheap motives. In no part of the kingdom do the Home Guard owe more than in Scotland to army aid and tuition. In the early days, before the force had found its feet or acquired the equipment it required, the army was a constant and reliable

source of encouragement and assistance. Officers and
N.C.O.'s from units stationed locally cheerfully gave up
their spare evenings to deliver lectures and demonstrations
to the L.D.V.'s. Officers home from Dunkirk came to
relate their experiences. Barracks were thrown open to the
Home Guard, and numerous courses instituted of a length
and character suitable to men not so fleet of limb as they
had once been and with civilian work to do in addition to
their soldiering. A battalion of the army would adopt a
battalion of the Home Guard. Long before the summer of
1940 was out field demonstrations of modern weapons and
modern tactics had been given. If the ex-Servicemen in
the Home Guard were pleased to be in company with the
new generation of soldiers the army looked upon the Home
Guard as its pupil. One of the most appreciated concessions
made by the War Office to the Scottish Home Guard was
permission to wear the Balmoral bonnet even though it did
cost each man 2s. 11d. If the War Office could soften its
heart for a second time and release from the twenty thousand
odd kilts it has in store enough to furnish forth the Scots
Home Guard pipe bands there would be no further serious
cause for complaint on the score of outfit.

A War Office school established in Scotland sends out
many travelling wings to coach Home Guard personnel in
every part of the country to the remotest islands of the
Hebrides. The school itself supplies a course of training
which, according to those who have been through both,
need not fear comparison with the instruction given by its
opposite number in England. It is certainly strenuous and
intelligent enough, and it has unquestionably inspired many
of the local training schemes which Home Guard zones
or battalions have put into operation. The school has also
been responsible, unwittingly, for what is probably the
best story relating to the Home Guard that has yet come
out of Scotland.

At one time the school was located in a mansion that had —in what might be called happier times—been part of a lunatic asylum. The Commandant, an Englishman, took special pains to point this fact out to the students at the beginning of each course. A few remnants of the earlier population of the building still clung to its neighbourhood, and wandered about the grounds, unperturbed by the detonations of sub-artillery and the racket of the whole canon of grenades. At one course, held during the worst of the great snowstorm of 1942, the students were returning from a sortie, ploughing their way, silent and weary, in the wake of their spry Instructor in Tactics, through a foot of snow, and hoping the canteen would contain enough to rectify the balance in frames not as young as they once were. As they neared the house they passed a small group of erstwhile patients. One of these, with a pitying glance at the column of speechless trainees, remarked to his companions, " Stupid b——s." When the course closed the students had been unable to make up their minds whether the man was daft or fey.

Another important school under the ægis of Scottish Command has, among other things, inspired the creation of schools in the big cities, especially intended for the teaching of street-fighting tactics. The result is that the Home Guard in Scotland is assured of a wide range of very advanced instruction, in which the urban battalions, far from being forgotten, receive particular attention. As the main battles in Russia have been fought in and around built-up areas, this is a wise precaution.

The great difficulty everywhere in the advanced training of the Home Guard is lack of time. A short week-end— from midday Saturday to evening Sunday—is the most that the majority of officers and N.C.O.'s can spare away from their business. But a nation that has solved the problem of compressing a first-class cricket match into an afternoon does not boggle at the task of making week-end tactical courses practicable. In at least one area, for example, there is an Active Service School, where Home Guards for twenty-four hours live at high pressure among rough country, with iron rations and only an hour or two's sleep. During the course they take part in three or four sorties. Rank is dispensed with. Anyone may command a section and be called upon at short notice to reach decisions of the utmost responsibility.

This Active Service School, the only one in the country for Home Guards, is located in a North Highland area. The " only begetter " is a regular army officer, a famous Rugby internationalist. The Commandant is a Home Guard officer. The whole twenty-four hours are spent at speed in country which is partly Highland, partly Lowland, in character. The hours of darkness are utilized, and usually a course has to be taken across the hills to a given objective in the darkness. A time-limit is set and, as a rule, although the march may be one of several miles and despite the not infrequently bad weather of the Highland foothills, it is seldom that the end of the journey is reached more than a few minutes late. All kinds of sorties are arranged, both in attack and defence. In short, a thorough training, limited only by the short time available, is given in tough country fighting. The school has been so successful that it was shifted in the autumn of 1942 deeper into the Highlands, and the course extended to a week, so that a special curriculum of instruction could be given to officers and N.C.O.'s.

Ordinary training in country warfare has never been difficult to get, since the British Army has always been keen on that very fascinating branch of tactics. Not so with town fighting, in which the Germans specialize, but which is not an object of enthusiasm in the British instructional canon. There are, however, three Home Guard schools of town fighting in Scotland, two of them—Aberdeen and

Glasgow—run by the Home Guard, while the third—in the Edinburgh area—is a Scottish Command School lent every week-end to the Home Guard. In these schools the Commandants, most of the instructing staff, and the demonstration squads belong to the Home Guard. The standard of toughness aimed at is probably higher even than in the Commando course already described. Lectures are given, during which the students are liable to be startled by thunder-flashes exploding near them. One test of presence of mind is that supplied by a student's progress through a house in which he is confronted in all sorts of unexpected places by sudden moving targets, at which he is supposed to fire. If he misses, or if he exhausts his magazine before reaching the last target, the student is very properly counted out. Instruction is given in the jumping of walls and the scaling of house-fronts by means of toggle-ropes. Cunningly camouflaged marksmen cover a route, and the student is expected to find them. (He never does.) A fortified and defended house has to be attacked, and in the ensuing battle, with smoke and din, the several ways of capturing or masking a fortified point are learned. In one of the schools it is claimed that they can make any man from seventeen to seventy agile enough to take his share in a street battle. Certainly men not far short of the higher of these age-limits have been seen making their way safely up the wall of a house by the aid of a toggle-rope.

The labours of these training centres are supplemented by the enterprise of Zone, Battalion, and Company Commanders everywhere. There may be an absence of uniformity in training throughout Scotland, but there is a great variety of ingenuity, and it is not unreasonable to argue, as a large number of Home Guard officers do argue, that the Boche is more likely to be beaten by the heterodox than by conventional methods which he knows about. And

H

whatever may be the case with the army, the experience of the Home Guard testifies to the inexhaustible capacity of the civilian soldier for taking instruction. A good story is told of an army lecturer who was talking to a Home Guard platoon in the Western Isles. Like most lecturers, he soon singled out his most attentive listener, whose intelligent eyes and mobile expression were a constant inspiration. At the end the lecturer commented to the officer in charge upon the attentive demeanour of this particular auditor. "That may be," was the reply, "but he is the only man in the platoon who doesn't speak English. Gaelic is his only language." There may be a moral lurking in that anecdote, not for the Home Guard only.

CHAPTER 9

Confessions and Impressions

THERE is no doubt in my mind that one of the most serious brakes on the efficiency of the Home Guard during the whole of its career has been and to some extent still is the attitude of the wives of its members towards their husbands' new interest. Generally speaking, wives were jealous of the Home Guard, and resented its call upon their husbands. In their view an enthusiastic Home Guard was a poor husband, because he invariably put the Home Guard first and his wife second.

This happened throughout the force regardless of financial or social differences. That trip to the pictures, that dinner-party, that game of golf, in fact, all the ordinary pleasurings of pre-war life could be and often were thrust aside in favour of a sudden call to Home Guard duties. So the sentence, " You cannot find time to take me out, but you can always find time for your old Home Guard," was heard from wifely lips in all sorts and conditions of homes.

Possibly there were two main reasons for this, one being that never before in living memory had Britain's civilians been under military orders, and the other that these semi-compulsory duties were unpaid. And yet, to the mystification of their wives, the Home Guard did them eagerly. Women, of course, and especially wives, are materialists ; they have to be. It is the men who are the romantics. Shepherd Yates put this point admirably one night in the Wheatsheaf.

" Wimmen," he opined oracularly, " be like that. They cain't understand their men obeyin' orders 'an

worrittin' awver a job wot got no aypence attached to
it."

Which was largely true. Very naturally women judge
everything by how it affects them personally. The Home
Guard robs them of some of their husbands' time, attention,
and interest, and so they hate it. Besides, it's the old
story—it can't happen here. Holland, Belgium, and
France had been invaded; Dutch, Belgian, and French
women had had their homes overrun by alien troops, and
continental women and children had been machine-
gunned on the roads. No matter, our women just can't
or won't even imagine such a thing happening in Britain.
They hate the Germans, and they loathe the war, but
most of them are convinced that some day somebody
will win the war, and that everything will be as it was
before, and also that this will happen without their silly
middle-aged husbands behaving like Boy Scouts.

The reason for this general attitude is that there are no
invasion memories in this country, for even the great-
grandfather in Britain has none. But on the Continent
a grandfather in every village almost can take his grand-
child on his knee, point to some spot near their home,
and say with truth, " Now I remember when the enemy
were hiding behind that wall, and I was back there with
my rifle." Fortunately such reminiscences have been
denied to us ; and so we all, men and women and children,
have a hard job to imagine that during recent years such
things have only been just round the corner, or rather a
few minutes' flying time away.

Of course, the general belief that " it can't happen
here " lost and gained ground according to the varying
fluctuations of the war danger. There is no doubt that
the almost continuous night bombing of Britain during
the winter of 1940–41 did much to destroy it. There
was hardly one night that a few bombs did not fall within

a few miles of everybody's home, and every one had friends or relatives in London and other bombed cities. This and the invasion scare in September 1940 did much to destroy the general complacency, and more and more Home Guard wives were forced to realize that at any moment their middle-aged husbands might be called upon to fight in actual battle. It also kept those same husbands up to scratch in their Home Guard training. But as soon as the regular bombing ceased much of the old complacency returned, and with it the wives' resentment against the call that the Home Guard made upon their husbands' scanty leisure.

However, nowadays in most platoons a squad of its wives guarantee to cook for the local Home Guard during exercises and also should active service come to pass. This arrangement works well ; and now that many wives have seen their menfolk on duty all night, and those same menfolk have enjoyed a hot breakfast at 0430 hours, the old trouble has largely disappeared.

Another big handicap has been the question of dress. That may sound rather childish, but throughout the history of the Home Guard this clothes question has caused more grumbles and more ill-feeling than any other. Grouses by one man as to why another obtained a serge uniform ahead of him were understandable, and in due course the reason for them disappeared ; but grouses by the rank and file concerning the way in which some of their officers dressed should never have been evoked.

Frankly, I have never been able to understand this lack of taste on the part of far too many officers in the Home Guard, the more especially because by every standard—military, social, and rural—most of them might have been expected to know better. Instead, it was all too obvious that some of them cared far more about establishing

their own social superiority than for the efficiency of the
Home Guard. Orders would be officially issued that
at some demonstration or training the dress must be the
regulation Home Guard issue. N.C.O.'s and men turned
up as ordered, but almost invariably one or two officers
would arrive clad in their old regimentals, pleading that
the issue uniform did not fit. A few would even omit
to carry respirators, and in far too many cases shoes were
worn instead of boots and anklets. Nothing in my
experience has infuriated the Home Guards who obeyed
orders more than this has done; and I know that those
officers who have been and still are guilty of such bad
manners have always failed to get the best from the men
under them. They do not seem to realize that the average
old soldier member is a man who, when he was demobbed
in 1919, vowed that never again would he subject himself
to any form of army discipline. But at the first sound
of the bugle he fell in prepared to obey orders, and
therefore was doubly entitled to expect all his companions
to do the same. I myself have seen fifty such men almost
mutinous at the sight of a Home Guard officer flaunting
his old uniform.

It seems to me that one of the great war-time handicaps
of Britain is that class loyalty transcends all others—
loyalty to country, wife, family, religion, ideals, everything. The mainspring of so many people's lives seems
to be to consider the defence of their social position to
be more important than anything else. All of us suffer
from this defect little or much, but a few retired army
officers seem to have it worse than most. They joined
the Home Guard because it was the obvious thing to do.
They wanted to see Hitler beaten; and to achieve that
they were willing to do a lot of unpaid work, and spend
quite a lot of money, always provided their rank and
social position were sacrosanct. In fact, in some cases it

would seem that winning the war is a trivial thing compared with the really important one of always establishing rank and position. So they disobeyed orders and wore their old uniforms, just to prove to everybody that once they had been colonels. In fact, some of them, if given a choice between a heaven minus all class distinctions and a hell that insisted on them, would definitely prefer the latter.

Anyway I am certain that this sort of thing is mainly responsible for the general dislike of the army in this country. I have heard it stated that this dislike is a legacy from Cromwell, but I disagree on the grounds that, like enemy invasion, anything Cromwellian has long passed from living memory. Further evidence in support of the theory that active dislike depends far more upon living memory than upon historical writings can be seen in connexion with famine. When I was a small boy the agricultural workers had received a vivid picture of the hungry forties from their grandparents, but to-day their descendants have no living impression of those bad old days. But to-day every town-dweller has some actual memory or a clear painting from living relations of the 1914–18 war, when townsfolk went hungry and farmers waxed fat. Hence the prevailing objection during pre-this-war days and also to-day to granting any prosperity to home farming. During this war there are no fortunes being made in farming, and so the old animosity is dying and, I hope, will be dead when this war comes to an end.

So my conviction is that the pre-war and present general dislike of the army, in contrast to a complete absence of this feeling towards both Navy and Air Force, is largely due to recent animosity and not to any legacy from Cromwellian times or any other period of history that is beyond living memory. In all fairness it must also be stated that the majority of retired officers have done much to reduce this during recent years, but there is no disputing that the recent sins and bad manners of a minority have been so blatant as to obscure the virtues of the majority almost completely.

Now that we have and are likely to continue to have a conscript army the post-war remedy seems to be simple, although threefold. Firstly, take away from all Service rank every vestige of automatic social kudos. Secondly, to compensate for that loss, double, if necessary treble, the pay of all ranks, so that any man can afford to take any rank. Thirdly, recognize Service rank for what it is—merely a label necessary for the efficient running of that Service, but one that is permitted only to active members of the Service.

Thus, when General John Smith retires, he must become Mr John Smith, a civilian; and there must be no suggestion in his or anyone's mind that he either sinks or rises to the civilian level. Admittedly, if he has done his Service job so well that the nation owes him some lasting recognition he should be given some honour, such as a knighthood, but always an honour that is also given to eminent civilians. But he must, if the army is ever to become popular in Britain, abandon his Service prefix when he ceases to be a member of that Service.

For the life of me I can see no valid objection to this. If the one-time general, now plain John Smith, possesses any qualities that entitle him to the respect and friendship of his civilian neighbours he will obtain those precious things in good measure. If he is the type of man who needs to retain his Service rank to gain them he will never gain them, and will not be entitled even to the lip-service respect that the present system obtains for him.

Again, whenever I see a news-reel showing the head of some democratic country dressed in ceremonial civilian clothes reviewing that country's fighting services on parade in full uniform, I am always thrilled at the sight, and my Home Guard experience has taught me very definitely that this is the correct procedure. There is, of course, another alternative for this job in democratic countries, which is for the reviewer to wear the dress of the particular Service that he or she is reviewing, be that Service army, navy, air force, fire brigade, or air-raid wardens, and the rest as occasion demands. If uniforms are important—and they are—for pity's sake let democracy insist on more uniformity in connexion with the public review of every national service. But, frankly, I prefer the former alternative.

Which is perhaps a digression, and one that will invite the accusation of class-consciousness and bitterness; but the continuance of the old system is a much greater crime, and I am certain that the suggested change would obtain a large majority of civilian and Home Guard votes in this country. However, in due course the War Office noticed the dress grievance that inspired this digression, and in early 1942 issued a definite order insisting on regulation dress for all ranks, and also forbidding the purchase of privately tailored uniforms, with the result that the Home Guard has since been a much happier force.

Here, in all fairness, mention must be made of the surprisingly sympathetic way in which the authorities in Whitehall have always managed the affairs of the Home Guard. I use the word " surprisingly," because every ex-soldier member of the force expected nothing but hide-bound army-style red tape, and every civilian member was certain that this would be the official treatment. But from the Director-General downward throughout his staff the curious and complex nature of this new army was recognized from the beginning.

For instance, apart from its military value, the Home

Guard infuriated the German High Command mainly for this reason. That any mere civilians should dare to suggest that they could become useful soldiers by training in their spare time was an affront to the German professional soldier. It was a definite let-down for the soldiering profession, and if it succeeded much of the social kudos and arrogance of that profession would undoubtedly disappear.

And, as one Home Guard Staff officer once said to me, " The German officer is by no means the only soldier who thinks like that. The same prejudice is to be found among professional soldiers in this country. So, in addition to dealing with your grouses, we " (meaning the Home Guard Directorate) " sometimes have to act as a buffer between you enthusiastic amateurs and a few narrow-minded professionals."

Thank goodness such prejudice in this country was never very widespread and soon disappeared. In the beginning it was a relic of the army snobbery that was held up to ridicule so beautifully by Mr Punch some years ago. In his issue, dated August 4, 1909, he published a drawing showing two ladies talking in a drawing-room :

WIFE OF CIVILIAN : " Any news of your sister ? "
COLONEL'S WIFE : " Oh, haven't you heard ? Such a sad thing—she's married a civilian ; but she's been *so* brave about it."

Well, if the Home Guard has done nothing else but destroy that sort of thing for good and all it will have been worth while.

However, one type of ex-regular officer member of the Home Guard has done and is still doing much to add to its general happiness. This is the man who quietly and unobtrusively helped the bewildered civilian Home Guard officers at every touch and turn. Goodness knows, they needed it, for this soldiering job was the most difficult one they had ever tried to tackle. I say that because I cannot think that my own experience was very different from that of thousands of others.

Anyway, the ex-regular Home Guard officer spared no pains to rub off my more obvious corners. He grinned happily when he suggested that while a farmer in civilian clothes might lounge with his hands in his pockets while talking to a Staff officer, it was rather better business for that same farmer in uniform to endeavour to play this weird military game according to the accepted rules. Also, he invariably did his best to cover up my mistakes and awkwardnesses.

Again, I disliked, and still do dislike, the idea of shouting orders at a body of men, but he taught me not only how to make a fair fist of this, but also why it was necessary.

" You've been brought up to think that politeness is always worth while, and should be the first consideration in dealing with your fellow-man. Which is perfectly correct in normal times. But when you are in charge of a body of soldiers on parade or engaged in active operations, for the time being they cease to be your fellow-men, but become soldiers under your direction—a very different proposition. And under those conditions there isn't time for ' Please.' "

I must have continued to look unconvinced, so he gave me the following illustration :

" Supposing you are lecturing to our Home Guard in the hall one night, and a German parachutist appears in the doorway with a tommy-gun trained on the company. If you say to Joe Toomer, ' I say, old chap, would you mind attacking that fellow,' Joe will have time to think out five perfectly good reasons why he should not obey. But if you bellow, ' Toomer, get at him,' most likely Joe will tackle that fellow on the instant without thinking.

It's the job that lays down the style of address, with no question of personal relationships. In short, when occasion demands it, orders must be snapped out, even bellowed, and so you, my son, must learn how to bellow them if you intend to do your job properly."

Another type, the ex-regular officer, now in the ranks of the Home Guard, did even more for me. His civilian work did not permit him to become an officer, and so as a private he accorded me, a civilian who knew nothing about my job, the fullest measure of respect. His willing work and cheerful manner did much to maintain and inspire discipline in all ranks. On parade he was a private soldier ; off parade he was a guide, philosopher, and friend. In short, he was, if not God's best, the Home Guard's best bet.

Frankly, I have never before come up against anything so difficult and nerve-racking as this soldiering business. I could and did learn the tricks of modern weapons, and I worried over the comfort and equipment of the men to such fashion that I was jokingly accused by brother officers of fast becoming a dry-nurse to them. But anything in the nature of parades or drill used to prevent me sleeping at nights. In fact, even now it is only by a continual effort of will that I can get it into my head when I am facing a squad of men that my right hand is, so to speak, their left. Presumably one needs to be caught young to manage this drill business properly without thinking.

Also, having lived my pre-Home Guard life in circumstances in which one said " Please " to intimates, employees, golf caddies, waiters, or rather to friends, to bark out orders was and still is repugnant to me. It makes me feel hot under the collar and rather ashamed of myself. Consequently, my habit in the Home Guard has been to avoid giving orders whenever possible, and to cut the necessary ones down to a minimum.

That method seemed to work all right at home in my own platoon, but when I had to take a detachment of it farther afield for training purposes in company with many other detachments I was obliged in some measure to copy the ruling fashion. But never will I yap " Left-left-left " at a squad of Home Guards in public. However, feeling rather worried over my deficiencies, I once asked an ex-soldier N.C.O. whether in this way I was letting down the platoon during these public appearances.

" Don't you worry," he chuckled. " You see, they all know that you don't know the first thing about this job, and also that you're worrying yourself sick about it like a B.F. So they'll forgive you anything. But if you start chucking your weight about, watch your step. One fine day you'll make a howler, and then every man jack of 'em will obey that order to the letter, even if it means marching into the river. You carry on, and remember the Home Guard ain't regulars ; they're Home Guard, and they've got everybody weighed up to a nicety."

Which is true, but even with all the help and encouragement that I received from every rank in the Home Guard I soon found that the work of a platoon commander was beyond me. To-day it is almost a whole-time job, and I was soon faced with the position that either the platoon or my civilian work must be grossly neglected, and that even to half-do both meant that my health broke down. So I have been forced to tell my superior officers that I must give up the platoon to a better man, and to request that I be demoted to private or whatever rank they decide I can now best fill. Thank goodness one can go up or down in the Home Guard for such sound reasons without losing face or causing inconvenience to anyone.

Moreover, there is no other solution. At different stages in the life of the Home Guard all sorts of men have been able to do some useful work for it ; but when any member has outlived his usefulness in any position, the wisest thing, in fact the only thing, for him to do is to realize this, act accordingly, and subsequently give both help and appreciation to those men who somehow manage to discharge the onerous duties of platoon commander properly. To repeat, in these days that is a whole-time job, and often means that the holder of this rank must either employ a secretary or burn the midnight oil himself at a desk. For, in addition to much mechanism, modern soldiering seems to require a dickens of a lot of paper.

But no matter how many ups and downs, disappointments and vexations, successes and mistakes, no man in the Home Guard to-day regrets his service in it. It has given us all a new interest, a lot of fun, and enabled us to value our friends and neighbours with uncanny accuracy. I, for one, would not have missed it for anything.

CHAPTER 10

No Possible Doubt Whatever

THIS chapter is an attempt to answer two pertinent questions. The first is, " What place in the national defence plan has this amateur force attained after two years of life ? "

In the beginning the rôle of the Home Guard was largely confined to observation and report, policing certain specific points, such as telephone exchanges, bridges, and so on, plus the continuous harassing of enemy troops in as much as its weapons permitted.

The general idea was that each unit of the Home Guard should defend its own village or small town. Inadequate road blocks were erected every few miles, and protected by pathetically fragile and useless sandbag redoubts and pill-boxes in all too obvious places. Then everybody was afraid of tanks, and every Home Guard was busy working out plans or making amateur bombs to scupper these dreaded vehicles.

Shep. Yates put the early position admirably when he outlined it to his cronies in the Wheatsheaf one evening.

" We be a proper suicide squad, I reckon. Lookeezee, 'tes this way. Jerry'll come along the main road wi' 'is tanks an' all manner o' stuff. 'Ee'll beat up the Home Guard at Telmark, Sutton Evias, Hudwell, Bunchford, Willcombe, Chamton, and then may be we in Wallop. But each village'll hinder he a bit. P'raps only ten minutes apiece. But zix villages'll mean a full hour. Be that time 'tes to be hoped as the regular strikin'-force'll be got going, and 'it 'im fur zix."

When imminent invasion became less likely this attitude

changed. All over Britain, Home Guards of every rank were thinking and saying that if the time ever came when German tanks were running up and down the roads the position would be well-nigh hopeless. Laymen though they might be with regard to modern war, they all realized that any enemy invader must obtain the use of inland aerodromes if he were to have any chance of success, and also that tanks could travel across country. Accordingly they put less faith in road blocks, pulled down many of their early sandbagged defences, and demanded weapons that could stop tanks, arguing firmly that in open country riflemen and machine-gunners would be helpless against the advance of such heavily armoured fighting vehicles.

When Crete fell they demanded that instead of playing about at village road blocks they should form part of a general plan for the defence of aerodromes. In fact, at this time I heard one Home Guard state openly that with one platoon of Home Guard he could capture any aerodrome any morning before breakfast. Whether our aerodromes were so weakly defended then I do not know, but there is little doubt that they were insufficiently defended, and that everybody heaved a sigh of relief when their defences were strengthened all over the country.

The next phase was for every Home Guard platoon to detail and train a mobile squad, ready to move out at speed to deal with any local landing of parachute troops. Defence, it was argued, was all very well, but the thing to do was to attack whenever opportunity offered. These fire-eaters were given their heads in the matter of mobile patrols, but each platoon was told firmly that their responsibility for observation and report must still be properly discharged.

The point about continuous observation and report during any period of active service perhaps should be stressed. From the moment when the Home Guard is called to action stations nearly every one of its platoon commanders will be expected to tackle jobs for which any regular army officer would demand at least double the number of men. During twelve-hour or even twenty-four-hour exercises these responsibilities can be, and usually are, adequately discharged by the Home Guard, because for such short periods the men can carry on with little sleep, and the platoon commander probably with no sleep at all. Tired as they may be, they know that the exercise will finish at a certain time. But neither invasion nor battles are timed to end at a given moment, and so the real thing will mean that they must plan their arrangements to enable them to be able to carry on indefinitely. In other words, the general plan of campaign must permit or rather insist that both men and officers get adequate sleep save when their post is being attacked by the enemy.

The smallest district in the comprehensive network of Home Guard defence is the platoon area. This may be of any shape according to local circumstances, but as a general rule its size will vary from perhaps four to twelve square miles. The wise platoon commander will be a man who, while being far from lazy, appreciates the opportunity to laze, the value of sleep, and the comfort of an absence of worry caused by wondering what will happen next. To obtain these aids to efficiency for himself and his men he will institute a continuous system of observation and report throughout his area, night and day, coupled with frequent contact with the scouts from other platoons on its north, east, south, and west boundaries. Also, despite the unpopularity which this may bring, he will so worry the platoon commanders of all adjacent platoons that they do the same. In this way at all times, save when an attack is imminent, he will be able calmly to carry on with his defence plan, secure in the knowledge that no enemy is in the neighbourhood of his area in any direction.

I

In fact, if he has tested and perfected these continuous scouting and contacting arrangements regularly during training, and selected and practised his N.C.O.'s each to be responsible for the various details of the platoon's plan, he will be able to rest himself both physically and mentally until news of probable attack, when he will give to that the best that in him lies. In contrast, the haggard platoon commander who does not know what is happening in his own and the neighbouring areas, and who in consequence has not slept, will be in no fit condition when the—in his case—surprise attack takes place.

So the present general plan seems to be this. The Home Guard must keep watch and report any enemy movements, but instead of small bodies of men spread all over a platoon area, thus making that area weak everywhere and strong nowhere, the disposition of men and arms must be exactly the reverse. In each platoon the men are to be divided into three classes—scouts and observers, a mobile well-armed patrol of active men, and a main force of middle-aged and possibly lame stickers. The first will keep watch and ward over the platoon's area, and make contact with scouts of adjacent platoons ; the second will be stationed in the chosen nodal point, but will be always ready to move out on the jump to deal with any enemy landings anywhere in that area ; while the third are to hold that nodal point to the last. Thus, in the event of invasion or parachute landings by enemy troops, each platoon will know what is happening, report it, take steps to deal with it, and be very strong in one point in its area. In that way the Home Guard can to-day provide a stable framework of defence in depth against any enemy attack. In that framework they will be responsible for information, and do the local stopping and worrying the enemy, dealing swiftly with any fifth-column activities. In that same stable framework the regular army will be able to stage and push home a strong and mobile counter-attack.

This force of part-time soldiers was the only solution to Britain's defence problem. To provide that necessary framework of defence in depth all over the country would have been impossible by the use of whole-time soldiers, as this would have required all and many more than every man in Britain, which would have meant an almost complete stoppage of production. But by the institution of her Home Guard there is no doubt that Britain has contrived to keep her factories busy turning out arms, equipment, ammunition, and other necessary goods, her fields producing necessary crops, and also every acre of this island defended by trained men.

By the coming of 1942 the Home Guard had become such an important factor in the Home Defence of Britain, more especially because the formation of a Second Front in Europe was now rapidly changing from a possibility into a probability, that further steps had to be taken to keep it up to strength. Its regular intake of volunteers now consisted almost solely of lads as they attained the age of seventeen, but this increase was being neutralized by the disappearance of the eighteen and a half year olds into the regular forces. Furthermore, age, infirmity, and the increasing hours of civilian work among its older members were steadily taking toll of its numbers. Somehow more men must be recruited.

So reluctantly it was decided to institute compulsion, and to conscript suitable men between the ages of seventeen and fifty into this force that up to date had been wholly volunteer in character. Truth must be told—even in 1942 in every town and rural district there were such men who had hitherto evaded all forms of volunteer part-time national service. Also in some districts there might be too many men in the Civil Defence services and too few in the Home Guard. The civilian man-power of the nation was to be sorted out and disposed according to local needs.

When this was first proposed it was thought that many Home Guards over fifty years old would resign ; because, coupled with the conscripting of new recruits, after a certain date a maximum of forty-eight hours per month at Home Guard duties was to become compulsory alike for both conscripts and the original volunteer members of the force. The main reasons why some of the older volunteers did wish to resign were two in number—firstly, because after having done nearly two years' voluntary work they resented any form of compulsion ; and secondly, because they were afraid that their age would make it difficult and well-nigh impossible for them to put in forty-eight hours monthly in addition to their civilian work.

However, as by this time most Home Guard units were commanded by the right type of officer, very few of the older volunteers did resign. It was pointed out to them that forty-eight hours' training per month was the *maximum* compulsory amount, and that the *actual* was left to the discretion of the officers. Therefore, personal hardship, health, infirmity, or any reasonable cause for non-attendance would be considered fairly in the future, provided notice of and reason for non-attendance was given to any man's section leader. As one platoon commander put it to his older brigade, " For goodness' sake don't feel trapped. Stay in the force and trust me to see you get a fair deal."

That same man, an ex-soldier, also pointed out that middle age need have no fear of not being able to play its part in the event of invasion.

" In the first place," he said, " our battle won't be of long duration. A week at the outside. And any of us can stand roughing it for a week. In the second place, you have to remember that in most battles it hasn't been the actual fighting that's taken it out of the soldier, but perhaps having to march twenty miles carrying full equipment to the scene of action. Well, we're here on the scene of our battle, and all we'll need to do will be to stay put and scrap."

So, as might be expected, his over-fifties stayed put in the force. Some of them offered to do more. They longed to see one or two of their slacker neighbours conscripted and volunteered to " stay up all night drilling the so-and-so's if need be." However, once again their officers pointed out that the new conscripts must be made welcome in order that the force should continue as a happy family, and so retain its military efficiency. Generally speaking, this has come to pass.

However, from the time service in the Home Guard became compulsory the efficiency of the force has depended in still greater degree on the tact and good sense of its local commanders. The change has also brought them and their N.C.O.'s a greatly increased volume of work in keeping attendance registers and granting exemptions from parade to members for cogent reasons. Here and there difficulties have occurred, usually in connexion with the rival claims of agricultural and Home Guard duties. For instance, the man who is doing seventy hours weekly as a milker or stockman on a farm obviously cannot be expected to attend all parades, especially as he works both Sundays and weekdays in his civil employment. Again, during harvest and haymaking few farm workers can find any waking time free for Home Guard duties. So hard-and-fast rules are worse than useless, and the wise platoon commander uses his common sense and his country sense in translating the regulations to suit local conditions.

But it is just as absurd for farming folk to argue that the Home Guard must *always* give way to farming, as for the officer to insist that Home Guard duties must *always* take precedence over farming and other civil employment. Both activities are necessary in these dangerous days, and the platoon commander who sets his non-farming men harvesting instead of parading on Sundays during August and September is often a far more efficient Home Guard officer than the strict martinet who insists on following regulations to the letter. The former will have few absentees among the farming members of his command during the winter training, and thus a far more efficient platoon than the latter.

This, I think, is now generally recognized, and as a result the compulsory system is working fairly comfortably. It was necessary to make this change; the compulsory factor does keep the slacker up to the collar; but it need not and generally does not press too hardly on the good volunteer of any age, or on agricultural or any other form of production.

For instance, in most exercises the Home Guard combines with every form of Civil Defence to stage most realistic total war. The men go on duty during a whole week-end, during which time they are fed by a team of their wives and daughters. Farm workers are detailed to leave the post at stated times to go back to the farms to perform essential work such as milking; and are ordered to report back at the post at stated times. Such practices are invaluable, for even in the event of invasion the milk supply and others must be kept going as long as possible.

But it is easy to outline the how and why of to-day's position of the Home Guard in the national defence scheme, and even easier to put on paper some of the details of the way in which this came to pass. What is not so easy is to find an answer to the second question: "How will the Home Guard, a force of part-time soldiers, acquit itself in actual battle?" However, the Home Guard's second birthday did give me some indication.

To mark the second anniversary of the Home Guard the King assumed the appointment of Colonel-in-Chief of the Force, and announced this in a special Army Order in the following words : " Whatever the coming year may bring, I know that the Home Guard will offer the fiercest resistance to any enemy that may set foot on these shores."

So with that backing I now dare to prophesy the answer to that second question, and in this fashion to find also that difficult thing—a finish to a book about an armed force that as yet has never been tried in the fire of actual warfare. To do this I must make a full circle back to my starting-point of May 1940.

About that time many villages and small towns in Belgium and northern France were captured by the Germans, even though the attack was sometimes confined to but one tank or even three or four motor-cyclist combinations. From what I can gather from actual eye-witnesses something like this happened.

The local butcher-boy arrived at the east entrance of a village and tumbled off his bicycle, very frightened and out of breath.

" German tanks," he panted. " German tanks coming this way."

Whereupon the inhabitants of that village hastily evacuated it on the west side. So successful and swift had the German advance been that almost the entire civil population was in the grip of a new disease—" tankitis "—and fled at the first news of enemy approach.

Some day, may be, the British counterpart of that French or Belgian butcher-boy will tumble off his bicycle on the outskirts of a British village, bearing similar news. But the inhabitants' reaction will be very different.

In every British village there will be thirty or forty Home Guards, many a trifle stout, a few greyheaded, one or two lame, and some young boys of seventeen.

" German tanks," the local butcher-boy will pant.
" German tanks comin' this way."

" Are they ? " will be the local Home Guards' reply.
" Why, they're the b——s we've been waitin' for."

Whereupon they will take their weapons and go forward
to meet the enemy.   They may or may not be successful
in their fight, but they will take steps immediately to
deal with the coming attack.   None will even consider
any other alternative.   There will be no " tankitis."   None
will flee their village on the other side.

Of that there is no manner of doubt, no probable possible
shadow of doubt, no possible doubt whatever.